THE PRIVATE EYE ANNUAL 2007

EDITED BY IAN HISLOP

Published in Great Britain by
Private Eye Productions Ltd
6 Carlisle Street, London W1D 5BN

www.private-eye.co.uk

© 2007 Pressdram Ltd
ISBN 1 901784 46 6
Designed by Bridget Tisdall
Printed and bound by
Butler and Tanner, Frome and London
2 4 6 8 10 9 7 5 3 1

THE
PRIVATE
EYE
ANNUAL
2007
EDITED BY IAN HISLOP

"Have you tried switching it off and then on again?"

Do Penguins Wear Trousers?

Exclusive extracts from Private Eye's best-selling book 'Do Wasps Eat Penguins?' (sale to date 24 million)

Q. Is it true that the wheelie-bin was invented by a Belgian?

A.P Rushton

A. Indeed. The first wheelie-bin was designed in Ostend in 1885 by a Walloon fisherman, Andre de Bruges, who used it to transport his daily catch of mussels to a local inn, L'Hotel des Amis de Frites. His prototype was simply a tall wicker basket, which he perched on a set of pram wheels borrowed from his daughter. His fellow fishermen, mostly Flemish, laughingly called it 'Le Walloonie Bin'. However, the then-mayor of Ostend Henri FlammeKucher spotted its potential as a mobile refuse container and marketed it under Le Wheelie-Bin de FlammeKucher. This name failed to catch on, and by 1910 FlammeKucher's son had dropped the family name, thus paving the way to the iconic municipal refuse receptacle in use today.

Sadly, Andre never benefited from his invention and died penniless in 1902. In 1985, to mark the centenary of this world-changing invention, one of Andre's descendents, a New York property developer, Dwight J

Brugheimer III, paid for a twice-lifesize statue of his great-great-great-grandfather to be erected in the main hall of the now-refurbished Ostend Moules Marché, where it continues to draw many visitors to this day. In 2002 the statue and its environs were classified by the EU as a European Heritage Site.

Q. Do penguins wear trousers?

B. Tisdall

A. Of course penguins don't literally wear trousers! That would be silly! But the very rare Trouser Penguin (Pinguis pantaloonensis) which inhabits the remote Corby peninsula on South Georgia has distinctive leg markings which make it look from a distance as if it is wearing plus-fours. Indeed to the early British explorer Sir Horatio 'Toppo' Thompson, who discovered the islands in 1854, the bird was known as the 'Plus-Four Penguin'. He wrote in his diary, "We have discovered today a species of penguin hitherto unknown to science. Its flesh was somewhat salty but was reminiscent of the turkey. A curiosity of this species is that at first sight it looks uncannily like a chap dressed for a round of golf.

Furthermore, its egg has a mottled shell, very like a golf ball." The Trouser Penguin, which was featured in David Attenborough's recent TV series Planet Penguin, has been placed by the UN on its Red Alert of Most Endangered Avian Species.

Q. Has Heimsteiner's theory of the collapse of the inert nucleid ever been formally proved?

S. Farrimond

A. It is true that when the Austrian physicist Neville Heimsteiner came up with his famous theory in 1924, many of his Cambridge colleagues doubted whether his simplified theorem $D-X^{13}=C^{10}$ actually explained the phenomenon he called 'parallel connectivity'. But the consensus among modern particle physicists, notably Rufus Firefly, Professor of String at Harvard, is that Heimsteiner's theory holds, so long as the constant C is greater than (that's enough theoretical science, Ed.)

Order your copy now from Eyebooks Direct or choose one from these companion volumes. 'Do Moths Like Custard?', 'Are Bluebottles Really Green?' and 'Can We Have Your Money Please?'

HOW THE LEADER IS PREPARING TO BOW OUT

AN ASTONISHING leaked memo reveals how his inner circle of advisers are planning the retirement of the man who for the past twelve years has dominated the world scene.

Under the personal supervision of Josef Goebbels, the Chief Oberspinmeister of the fast-crumbling Hitler regime, the Führer's staff have been preparing for months a programme of carefully choreographed events which will allow their leader to end his career in a blaze of glory.

The document, which has been declared as "100 percent authentic" by the late Lord Dacre (Hugh Trevor-Ropey), sets out in meticulous detail how the Führer's closest advisers wish to see him leave the stage "on a high", with his reputation and dignity intact.

Reichstag At Bay

The main theme of the planned extravaganza will be "The Triumph of Nazism".

According to the memo, *"AH must be seen to be stepping down from office in a way which leaves the crowds wanting more.*

"When the curtain comes down and AH takes his final bow, the audience must be on their feet shouting encore, encore."

Dr Goebbels goes on to propose a series of high-profile media events designed to show the departing Führer not just as one of the greatest war leaders in history, but also as a truly caring father of his people, who loved Jews and gypsies.

"AH should be booked in now for

a full-length interview on Lord Haw Haw's popular Germany Calling show.

New Labour Camp

"AH should be invited to appear on Marching Songs of Praise, to introduce a selection of his favourite military music.

"AH should then go on a triumphal tour of what's left of our great German cities, such as Hamburg, Cologne and Dresden."

The memo acknowledges that *"the Second World War continues to cast something of a shadow over the Fuhrer's record in office,"* but Dr Goebbels describes this as *"the elephant in the bunker, which has to be exterminated by any means."*

The memo concludes *"Are we up to it? Is AH up to it? Perhaps the final solution will be for AH to win the sympathy of the world by some dramatic and heroic act, such as shooting himself. Only in this way can we stop Evil von Brown taking over, and will the thousands years of Blairism live on for ever."*

"And you've never considered having this piece of shrapnel removed, Grandad?"

THAT ALL-PURPOSE HEALTH SCARE PIECE IN FULL

YES, today's teenagers are becoming dangerously fat/thin.

Thanks to the pressures of modern life, health chiefs fear an epidemic of obesity/anorexia which will see our youngsters falling victim to a fatal desire to eat too much/too little.

If we don't do something now to make kids eat more/less, we are storing up a terrible crisis for ourselves in the very near future.

Our message to Britain's youth is simple. Keep/stop eating for God's sake.

© *All newspapers*

EXCLUSIVE TO THE DAILY MAIL

The world's greatest military historian, **Sir Max Hastings**, reports from the war they are saying we cannot win

I SEE OUR BOYS GO IN

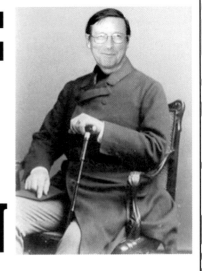

Balaclava,
Thursday October 25, 1854

I AM sending this report from the front line, where I have been spending time with our boys who are fighting for freedom and democracy in the inhospitable terrain of the faraway Crimea.

And let me say at once that I take my hat off to the gallant lads of one of Britain's finest regiments, the Light Brigade.

They may have been asked to carry out an impossible task, with wholly inadequate forces and equipment.

But make no mistake, morale is high. Says the bluff, moustachioed British Commander, General Sir 'Cardy' Cardigan. "We have been given a job to do and we're jolly well going to do it.

"Of course, numerically

we're a tad short. I freely admit that we've only got 600 men and 600 horses, when ideally we could use 50,000 of each if we're going to teach those Russkies a lesson.

"But I am sure the 600 will not let the side down when we send them in to the so-called 'Valley of Death'."

When I put it to the General that the politicians in London had sent them on a hopeless mission for political reasons, 'Cardy' Cardigan fixed me with a steely blue eye and replied, "I'm no politician. I'm a simple soldier. And if they tell me to send 600 men to their deaths as a futile gesture, that's what we're trained for."

ON OTHER PAGES: Frontline report (in verse) by our 'embedded' poet Alfred Tennyson. **16**

Her Majesty The Queen On Meeting Jeremy Paxman

IT IS with a feeling of some dread that one approaches the iconic figure of Jeremy Paxman who has for so many years held a unique position in our national life.

We are not naturally an admirer of the institution of Newsnight, with its overpaid courtiers and its code of deference towards Mr Paxman, but undoubtedly, for millions of people, Paxman is a symbol of hope and comfort, standing above politics as he does, offering from his palatial office in White City an impartial, wise perspective on the affairs of this country.

Paxman has seen Prime Ministers come and go and has proved that he has an immense amount of experience to offer.

However, actually seeing him in the flesh was a nerve-racking experience even for a cynical old monarch like ourselves.

He is taller than he appears on television and much more friendly than you would think.

He said to me, "It is an enormous pleasure to meet you, your Royal Ma'amship," and laughed uproariously when I sneered at him and said "Come off it!".

After spending some time with him, we have had to change our opinion somewhat and concede that Jeremy Paxman is a good thing for Britain. And the alternative is surely unthinkable. Kirsty Wark? We think not.

© *Abridged extract from "Vivat Paxman!" by Queen Elizabeth II.*

IT'S A BIT YOUNG FOR YOU

THE DAILY TELEGRAPH

BEANO BORIS APOLOGISES TO THE PEOPLE OF PAPUA NEW GUINEA

CRIPES! Old Boris has really put his foot in the cooking pot this time! Blimey – fancy me saying that the chaps in the Labour Party (BOO!!) were behaving like cannibals in Papua New Guinea!

No wonder they got shirty! Even jolly old cannibals don't like to be compared to the ghastly crew running the show in Blighty! No, friend cannibal has taken offence at being called a "Missionary Muncher" and says that nowadays they're all decent, civilised coves, many of whom went to good schools like me and my friend Dave and belong to clubs like Whites – even though they're black!!

Anyway, old Bozzer has got to eat his words (oo-er!!), otherwise one of the cannibal johnnies will come round here and eat **me** for breakfast!

© *B. Johnson, MP for Henley and Shadow Minister for Higher Education.*

TARRANT SHOCK

I boned a friend...

Letters *to the Editor*

SIR – The critics of Pope Benedict XVI's recent lecture at the University of Katzenrausschpielenmaus have entirely missed the point of his scholarly reference to the words uttered in the 12th century by the little-known Byzantine emperor Obscurus III. When Obscurus said that "these Muslims are blood-thirsty villains who are up to no good" ("non bono Islamici sunt", as he put it in the original Greek), what he clearly meant to say was that there was "a window of opportunity for dialogue between our two great faiths at this moment of heightened tension in the Holy Land". To interpret the emperor's words in any other way is a deliberate attempt to exacerbate an already fraught situation.

Dr Nathaniel Beardsworth
Dept. of Byzantine Studies, the University of Doncaster.

SIR – Surely the Pope should be looking first at the plank in his own eye, ie the long record of Islamophobic genocide which has characterised the entire bloodthirsty history of the Christian church ever since it began, right down to the latest crusade led by the neo-con, born-again Blair and Bush in their attempt to destroy Islam, just as their predecessors did when they invaded the Holy Land in search of oil in the Middle Ages.

The Right Rev. David Spart
Dean of Theology, Oxford University.

SIR – Re: the recent comments by His Holiness – is this what they mean by "Papal Bull"?

Mike Giggler
Via email.

● Listen to a podcast of the Pope's recent controversial lecture in full, as read by Stephen Fry, then text us with your views on 84611 on www.telegraphbust.com

GERMAN POPE SHOCK APOLOGY

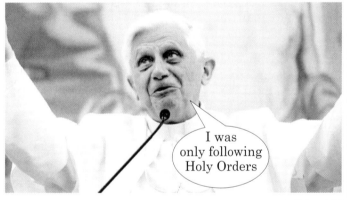

I was only following Holy Orders

A Cabbie writes

EVERY week a well-known taxi driver is invited to give his views on an issue of national importance. This week: the **Pope**'s views on Islam by Kevin Snott (Cab No. 1234).

Don't get me wrong, guv, I've got nothing against Catholics. But that Pope hasn't done himself any favours, shooting his mouth off like that about the Muslims. I mean it was obvious that they were going to get the hump and go mad. The man's a complete and total idiot. Mind you, he's got a point of course. I mean, just look at them, those Muslims, blowing themselves up and trying to kill everyone. You can hardly call that "peace-loving", can you? No, give the Pope a medal, that's what I say. It's time someone had the guts to stand up and say what he said, though he shouldn't have said it. What a fool! I had that Abu Hamza in the back of the cab. I asked him for a tip and he said, "Convert to Islam or I'll cut your head off"! Very clever man...

Next week: Eddie Bung (Cab No. 442) on the future of English football.

How dare the Pope say we are a violent religion?

TRINITY OF EVIL: CHRISTIAN CRUSADE AGAINST ISLAM

Let's kill him

How do you react to the analysis of Islam as a religion spread by military conquest?

ISLAM WILL CONQUER ROME

We're up in arms

STEVE IRWIN 1962-2006 R.I.P.

R.I.P.

P.W. BOTHA

WHITE MOURNERS ← → BLACK MOURNERS

BIRCH

STRICTLY BALLROOM

YAAAY! PINOCHET'S DEAD!!!

Latest Latin-American Dance

EXCLUSIVE TO THE EYE

BLUNKETT'S LAST TAPE

EXCLUSIVE extracts from the sensational book and television programme that is in all other papers as well

THROUGHOUT my political life my main concern has been to keep my private life private. This was particularly important when I was occupying the most senior position in the government and taking tough decisions that affected every single person in the country.

It was obviously vital that no one should know I was cracking up because then the public would have had no confidence in me and would have demanded that I be sacked.

September 2004

NO ONE has ever suffered as much as me. I have probably suffered more than anyone in the whole world has ever suffered. My suffering makes the First World War look like a vicarage tea party. And a particularly enjoyable one at that. The media are behaving like East German SS Guards. When I got home a photographer from the Sun was waiting for me. "Give us a smile, David," he demanded. "You try smiling when you are suffering more than anyone else has ever suffered," I shouted back.

Perhaps I was wrong to describe all my colleagues as "useless idiots" in a book by Stephen Pollard. But why do they hate me? What have I ever done to them? At least some people were sympathetic.

October 2004

AT a reception in honour of the proprietor of the Daily Star I meet Prince Charles who offers kind words.

"We've all had affairs with other people's wives and had to go through hell. I really sympathise with myself."

What a great man he is. No wonder he is so popular with everyone in the country. Unlike John Prescott and Jack Straw who I really hate. But why do they hate me? Don't they know how much I am suffering?

After the terrible events that led to my unfair resignation which made the Second World War look like another vicarage tea party – only this time with jelly and custard to make it even more enjoyable – I spoke to the Prime Minister.

December 2004

Tony hugged me and wept. "We cannot do without you, David, but you are fired." He has always been my greatest supporter except when he had to fire me. I left his office feeling a weight of suffering equivalent to the entire history of mankind. It makes the Third World War look like a vicarage tea party, except one with Lemon Drizzle Cake and *(cont. p. 94)*

© *Fishwick and Tweed £19.99*

TOMORROW: How dare the media invade my privacy when I want to sell it to Bloomsbury and get my share of the Harry Potter gold?

CHARLES IN BOILED EGG DRAMA

Where are my soldiers?

They're all being killed in Iraq

"He has an irrational fear of identity theft"

CAKES TOPS FEE LEAGUE
'I'm so proud,' says Head

by Our Education Staff **John Mortarboard**

A DELIGHTED Mr Kipling was today celebrating the triumph of the prestigious Midlands independent school, St Cakes *(Motto: Quis Paget Entrat)*, in the league tables for the Country's Most Expensive Schools.

Even Eton at £25,000 per week could not match the £1million a term that St Cakes demands of its pupils. Dr Kipling was quick to praise the Bursar, Wing Commander von Hoogstraten (O.C), for his part in raising fee standards to the current level.

"St Cakes is now so successful that pupils are fighting to get in – literally so in the case of some of the Russian oligarch parents and the warlords from Central Africa."

"Of course we still have some British parents but they find it increasingly hard to match the high quality of money from overseas."

ST CAKES FACT FILE

Alumni include:

Sir Stephen Fry
(Baftas, 1972-1979)

Jordan
(Crumpets, 1995-1996)

Sir Alan Sugar
(Amstrads, 1962-1966)

Conrad Black
(Chokeys, 1954-1959)

Jeffrey Archer was *never* at St Cakes though in his Who's Who entry he claims to have been Head Boy.

First Computer to Edit National Newspaper

By Our Media Staff **Phil Blog**

THE DAILY TELEGRAPH yesterday became the first British newspaper to be edited by a computer.

Known as the 'DT3PO', the state-of-the-art machine will perform all the functions which used to be carried out by human editors, including sacking journalists and making sure that the pages are correctly numbered.

PC World

Last night, speaking from his desktop in the Telegraph's new 'IT Centre' over London's Victoria station, the computer told the Eye: "this is very exciting... enter password... meeting the challenge of the digital age... podcast... webcam... Simon Heffer... exterminate, exterminate... I will obey the Barclays."

Unfortunately the computer crashed before we were able to ask it "Is it true that all your writers and readers have gone off to the Daily Mail?"

■ *You can download the full version of our exclusive interview with DT3PO into your iPod at www.goodbyetel.com*

WHERE HE STANDS – CAMERON SPELLS IT OUT

by Our Man In Bournemouth
Matthew D'Anconservative

THEY said he was all style and no substance. But yesterday Tory leader David Cameron proved them wrong, with a wide-ranging set of firm commitments which staked the ground on which he will fight and win the election.

Here are the bold, rock-solid pledges that mark out the Cameron agenda as forged in steel.

MARRIAGE

"The Tory party is firmly committed to the institution of marriage. It is the bedrock of our society. And, of course, by the term 'marriage' I include civil partnerships between same sex partners, co-habitees, single parents and anyone else trying to bring up children or just living alone watching television."

THE HEALTH SERVICE

"The greatest British institution of them all. The Tory Party will defend the NHS against everyone who is opposed to it. We will resist any further attempts by this government to involve the private sector, except, of course, when it's needed, which it often is, and then, of course, we are right behind them."

THE ENVIRONMENT

"Everyone is now agreed that the most important issue confronting mankind is the environment. Unless urgent action is taken now by the entire world, we face the prospect of massive global warming, ice caps melting, polar bears swimming for their lives and some of us no longer able to take holidays in the Maldives because they are under water. We've got to stop flying around the world and go on our bikes instead. So committed are we to this that a Conservative government will look into giving a tax break to every family which installs a wind turbine on its bicycles to power their lights."

EUROPE

"No one's interested in this."

IMMIGRATION

"Ditto."

IRAQ

"We are right behind our Armed Forces who have a difficult job to do and do it jolly well." *(Pause for applause)*.

AMERICA

"The Conservative Party is pledged to be in full support of George Bush, but we reserve the right at all times to criticise him. We will never give in to knee-jerk anti-Americanism, but we must also be aware of the dangers of slavish pro-Americanism. Was it not the great Senator John McCain who yesterday said I was 'the JFK of today' and you can't get fairer than that!"

TAX CUTS

"The Conservative Party has always stood for lower taxes, unless of course it is necessary to have higher taxes, in which case it would of course be the height of irresponsibility to commit ourselves in advance to saying whether taxes should go up or down."

BORIS

"Aren't we lucky to have him, so that nobody bothers to analyse what I am saying too closely! Thanks, Boris!"

(Prolonged laughter and headlines)

THE LABOUR GOVERNMENT

"We shall continue to support the government whenever we believe that what they are doing is in the interests of the country, which is why I shall be voting for them at the next election."

Lives of the Saints

No. 94 St David of Cameron And The Killer Jellyfish
by award-winning historian **Brother Andrew of Roberts**

And there was living in those days a much-revered young monk named myself. And on one fine afternoon this admirable scholar had it in mind to take a healing dip in the ocean.

Imagine his horror when suddenly there manifested itself from the deep a mighty throng of deadly jellyfish, a hideous green in colour and some of them many feet across.

Brother Andrew was sore afraid as he saw these monster leviathans bearing down on him, their tentacles poised to fill him with lethal venom.

At just that moment, watching from the shore was a young nobleman of that country who witnessed the monk's plight with deep compassion. It was the blessed David of Cameron.

And David did not hesitate, but cast himself into the waves, determined to save Brother Andrew from a watery death.

No sooner had he reached the hapless victim, struggling for his life, than the jellyfish swam away in terror, never to be seen again.

And David placed Brother Andrew on his back and took him gently and safely to the shore.

And many years later, when this story was revealed to the world by Brother Andrew, the people of that land were amazed and said with one accord, "We don't believe it. You've just made it up to crack up your old mate David, to make us think he is a saint and should be prime minister."

"That is not true," replied Brother Andrew. "I have told this story only to get some publicity for my new book."

Brother Andrew's new book 'A History of the Anglo-Saxon Speaking Peoples' is published this week by Snipcock and Tweed at £25.99.

GREEN TORIES

"Um... perhaps we need to stress the green a little more, and the Tory a little less"

DIARY

VICTORIA BECKHAM: MY FASHION SECRETS

Why is a T-shirt called a T-shirt? That's a question David and I often ask ourselves.The conclusion we've come to is that it's because it's a shirt. Otherwise, it would be called the T-trouser or T-shoe, or whatever.

Buying a T-shirt is one of the most difficult decisions any of us will ever be faced with. There are just so many different ones to choose from, I really don't know how I manage, but over the years I've succeeded time and time again. I suppose I just put it down to experience. But it's a skill that ordinary people can pick up too, if they're prepared to listen.

When you're planning to enter a fashion shop to buy your T-shirt, be sure to check that the door is open else you could give your head a nasty bang. If you find that the door is shut, my advice is to give it a push with your hand, or, better still, get your personal assistant to push it for you. Who wants a girl with great big muscley arms? Certainly not my David!

The whole shop may be closed because it's not opening hours or whatever. This can be very inconvenient, especially if you're already rushed off your feet with your career and family, so best ask your agent to phone them in advance and get it to specially open for you.

VICTORIA'S TOP TIPS: If you crave a pair of new shoes, be extra careful not to go to a shop which sells only lingerie or woollens. Look for signs saying "shoes". If you really don't feel like going shopping at all, my advice is to leaf through fashion magazines until the mood passes. If the problem persists, consult your doctor.

So now you're safely through the door, you'll find the T-shirts in the T-shirt section, that's unless they've moved them for some reason without telling you. I once wasted a whole lot of time struggling into an evening gown because the T-shirt section had been moved and no-one had bothered to inform me, thank you very much.

Once you have successfully located the T-shirts, you must pick one that is your size and suits you. If you are very very large, you shouldn't pick one out that's marked VERY VERY SMALL because it probably won't fit.

My mum always taught me that to wear clothes which are in your size, because that way they'll fit better. It's a lesson I've stuck to ever since. Unless I want, say, a really big woolly jersey, in which case I'll go for one that's bigger, so that it looks bigger when it's on.

VICTORIA'S TOP TIPS: Can't find exactly what you're looking for? Put a call through to your friend top designer Roberto Cavalli and get him to make one for you.

Most top designer shops and high-street fashion stores have dressing rooms specially set aside for customers to try clothes on in. If you find there already other people in them trying clothes on, don't worry, just get your assistant to have a word with the store manager and she'll get them removed.

It's funny, but dressing rooms often have mirrors on their walls. For a long time, David and I wondered why this was. David thought it might be so that you could see if anyone was behind you, but we were told by a top fashion expert that it was so that you can look at yourself in your new clothes before buying them, which is a really great tip to pass on.

VICTORIA'S TOP TIPS: Good does not necessarily mean expensive. It's how you feel inside that's important. I am just as happy slobbing around in a £95 frock from a high street chain inside, then I'll change into something more stylish before going out.

Picking a T shirt may not be easy but trying it on is even more difficulter.

Basically, a well-made T-shirt generally comes complete with four holes. There's a medium-sized hole for putting your head through, two smaller ones for putting your arms through and then there's big one which is basically for your body. If you get it wrong by just a matter of inches and try putting your head through an arm-hole, you could end up in intensive care, so whatever you do you must be careful to aim right.

And that's not all. The other nightmare is finding you've put it on back-to-front. If that ever happens to you, my top tip is to get your assistant to take it off for you, then put it on you again, only this time the right way round.

Alternatively, you can try taking your arms out through the holes, then turn your T-shirt round 180 degrees, then put them back in again. Sometimes David makes the major mistake of turning it round 360 degrees and then he gets cross when he finds it's still the wrong way round.

Congratulations! You have now bought a fantastic super-sexy new T-shirt! When you get it home, be sure to try it on. That way, you get to enjoy it at least once before it seems old and boring, and you have to go shopping again for something newer.

As told to CRAIG BROWN

Nursery Times

························· October 27, 2006 ·······························

GENERAL SAYS 'IT'S TIME TO PULL OUT'

by Our Defence Staff **Captain Corelli's Barnet**

THE Grand Old Duke of York today defied the government in an astonishing break with constitutional protocol.

To Hill and Back

The Duke, commanding ten thousand men involved in Operation Hill Freedom, said, "It is time to admit that marching up to the top of the hill was a strategic error and we have to accept the only military option left to us, i.e. marching down the hill as soon as possible."

The Duke of York said, "Look let's be honest. When we were up, we were up. And when we are down, we will definitely be down. But currently we are

in a situation where we are only half-way up and so are, frankly, neither up nor down – which I have to say is unsustainable."

On Other Pages

● Tagged Goldilocks Reoffends with Second Bear Break-In **2** Old Woman Adopts African Baby **3** No More Stocks of Fishy on Little Dishy Shock **94**

New Words

●●

Opposition (*n.*) body of persons who agree with the government. Example: "Her Majesty's Opposition is committed to wholehearted support of Mr Blair's excellent administration on all issues" (D. Cameron, Hansard, 2006).

Leader of the Opposition (*n. insubstantive*) person who is even more in agreement with the government than his colleagues. Example: "I want to be the new Blair" (D. Cameron, dinner party, 2006).

General (*n.*) person who now fulfils role of Leader of the Opposition. Example: "The government's policy has totally failed, says General" (Sarah Sands, Daily Mail, 2006).

"Oi, David!" called Princess Posh. "Where's that pea I was saving for my lunch?"

STRAW 'NO TO VEIL'

How dare you show your face round here?

Hussy

Russell.

PRESCOTT SHOULD WEAR VEIL – MUSLIM WOMEN SPEAK OUT

by Our Islamic Staff **Michael Buerqua**

REPRESENTATIVES of the Muslim Community today demanded that John Prescott should cover his face completely when meeting them in person.

Said spokeswoman Tamsin Yashmak, "As a sign of respect, Prescott should wear a mask. It is difficult to hold a serious conversation with him when you have to look at his large, bloated, sweaty face."

Women Should Not Wear Veil Or Anything Else – Prescott Spells It Out

Full story plus pix **8**

Daily Telegraph Gets Rid Of Sub-Editors

By Our Graduate Trainee Phil Blogs

IN A move to increase efficiency at its new headquarters in Victoria, the Daily Telegraph newspooper has decided to dispose with sab-editers.

Said one of the Barclay Twains, "We have no nude for sobs here. They are expansive and a waist of tome. Our reporting stiff can do the jab unstead."

The Barclay Twits are 198. *(Please check. Oh, sorry, I forgot there aren't any subs.)*

GLENDA SLAGG

THE GAL THEY CAN'T VEIL!!!!!

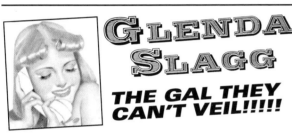

■ HATS OFF to superstar Madonna for saving the life of baby David!?! The world's top pop icon has done her bit for Africa by plucking one tiny helpless toddler from certain death in malaria-infested Malawi and taking him off to a new life where he'll never have to worry about where the next meal is coming from. God bless Madonna, for proving that she is the Mother Teresa of rock-'n-roll!?!!

■ MADONNA. WHO does she think she is, the Mother Teresa of rock-'n'-roll?!? How dare she swan off to Africa to buy someone else's baby as if it were just a designer handbag from Prada!?! Take it from me, Madge, baby David needs your so-called charity like a dose of Malawi-infested malaria!? Have you ever stopped to think what a life of lonely misery this poor little boy will have, as you go jetting round the world, a-struttin' and a-ruttin' on the stage. Let's face it, what little toddler wants to see his mum crucified in suspenders in Wembley Stadium!?! Take him home, Grandma, but don't ask for your money back!!!?!

■ SPARE A thought for poor old Macca!! His mad missus has cooked up a pack of lies in order to get her hands on all his millions. So he beat you up!! Who wouldn't?? It's amazing he put up with you so long, a-shoutin' and a-poutin', a-whingein' and a-cringin', a-squealin' and a-stealin'. Want to know what I think?? I think you should get half of nothing. And even that would be too much. Go on, hop it!!?! (Geddit??) *(Keep going. Ed.)*

■ SO, MACCA'S a drunken monster who beats up his missus. I knew it all along!!?! You only have to look at him to see that, beneath the boyish good looks and cheery charm, he's Jack the Ripper and Reggie Kray all rolled into one!!?! I hope she takes him for every penny he's got, and even that won't be enough!!?!

■ *HERE THEY are – Glenda's Halloween hunks!?!!*

● **Jacob Rees-Mogg!?!!** He's a snob and a lunatic, just like his Dad. Mmmmm!?!!

● **Bill Oddie?!??** TV's Mr Naturist. You've certainly got an eye for the birds?!! Have you ever thought of coming a-twitchin' round my place!?? I'm over here, Bill, tweet tweet!!?!

● **Alan Bennett!?!??** OK, so I know you've got a history with boys (Geddit?!!?), but I'm sure we can work something out!?!

Byeeee!!!

"There – isn't that better? A nice family meal together for once"

– PILBROW –

HEATHER MACCA LATEST

NOW THE GLOVES ARE OFF!

by Our Showbiz Correspondent
Biff Bamigboye

IT'S shaping up to be the dirtiest and most titanic divorce battle ever as the two sides yesterday came out of their corners to fire the opening salvoes in what promises to be the biggest war-to-the-death in the history of the world *(see Eye wall chart of Great British Divorces)*.

Here are Heather's ten devastating charges against her Beatle billionaire soon-to-be ex-husband.

● he put rat poison in her goldfish bowl.

● he refused to buy her a jumbo-jet for Christmas.

● when the Peasmarsh Echo called her a "gold digger" he refused to hire a hit man to take out the editor.

● he frequently snored at night so loudly that she couldn't concentrate on her Sudoku.

● he put her pet rabbit in the microwave just like in that film.

● he tried to stab me in the shower just like in that other film.

● he kept going on about the Beatles as if anyone cared.

● he made me listen to his new album even though he knew I was disabled.

● he more than once left his trousers lying on the floor instead of folding them up and putting them in the trouser press like I told him to.

● when I told him his new oratorio* was rubbish, he pulled a long face, which was very hurtful considering that I was disabled, and wouldn't speak to me for the rest of lunch.

Mr McCartney's solicitors Messrs Twist and Shout hit back by refusing to comment.

* Ecce Cor Blimey © Classic-FM

LEAVE DADDY-LONG-LEGS ALONE!

 Says award-winning columnist MAX HASTINGS

EVERYWHERE I go, I'm hearing people complaining about a plague of junk mail. *(That was last week. Ed.)*

I mean, of course, daddy-long-legs. But what harm have these delightful creatures, with their gossamer wings and spindly elongated legs, ever done to anyone?

And what could be more charming than to sit round the table with one's children, while these friendly visitors flit gaily round the room like so many elegant ballerinas? *(Keep going. Ed.)*

Unlike the hated wasp, these silent sexto-pods do not attempt to inflict painful stings upon us at the slightest excuse.

Unlike the menacing blue-bottle, they do not give off an infuriating buzz in the hope of driving us mad. *(More of this. Ed.)*

It is the tiresome moth which keeps one awake at night, when one is trying to read in bed – not our agreeable friend the crane-fly.

It is the killer bee which every year wipes out entire communities in Sub-Saharan Siberia *(Please check, subs.)*

Meanwhile your good old-fashioned British daddy-long-legs reminds us of our childhood and the England that we used to know and love – warm beer, the village cricket pitch, dead pheasants falling like autumn leaves out of the October sky, and the welcome ring of the telephone as the editor of the Daily Mail calls up to offer me £1,000 a word for more of this rubbish.

FREE with tomorrow's Daily Mail, the great British Daddy-Long-legs Wallchart.

LAST TESCO FOR 400 YARDS

TESCO

The Alternative Rocky Horror Service Book

No. 94 A Revised Service of Matrimony

The President *(for it is he or she)*: Brethren and sistren (but mainly sistren). We are gathered here together to join this unhappy couple in the state of deadly matrimony, which is an estate ordained by a patriarchal God and greatly to be feared.

All: Too right!

President: Do you, N or M *(here he or she may say Shane or Rhiannon or similar)* really want to go ahead with this, given the likelihood that it will lead to domestic violence?

N & M: If you put it like that, we may have to give it another thought.

President: For does it not say in Holy Scripture that a man shall leave his parents and beat up his wife?

N or M: Oh, no one mentioned that before.

President: Do you, M, really want to "honour and obey" some man who will use this as an excuse to beat you black and blue every time he's been out for an evening drinking with his mates, which is what all men do, frankly, unless they're gay, of course, in which case we should be ordaining them rather than marrying them?

All: Ha ha ha!

President: In the light of the above, do you hereby renounce the evil of marriage and determine to lead a new life in holy cohabitation?

N & M: I think we're well out of it.

(Here the congregation shall sing a hymn, possibly "Fight The Good Wife With All Thy Might" or "Don't Abide With Me [I Can't Abide You Either]")

The Dismissal

President: I hereby dismiss marriage as an outdated, sexist plot designed to keep women in a state of perpetual submission by use of such patriarchal stereotypical language as "Lord", "Father", "Mankind", "Husband" etc, which to my mind is frankly sickening and has led to thousands of years of wives being murdered and raped in the name of so-called Christianity.

All: Indeedy-doody! Tell it like it is, sister!

Recessional

(The unmarried couple shall then not sign the register and shall leave the church, accompanied on the organ by some suitable voluntary, such as "I'm Not Getting Married In The Morning")

TYRANT'S LAST APPEAL

Get me Lord Hutton!

News In Brief

HATED TYRANT SENTENCED TO 'HANG AROUND'

THERE were scenes of jubilation in Washington today as hated former President George Bush was sentenced by his people at the mid-term elections to "hang around" for the next two years as a powerless leader who *(cont. p. 94)*

SADDAM VERDICT TO GIVE BUSH ELECTION BOOST

I'm hoping for a big swing

DAILY ✠ EXPRESS

THE WORLD'S GREATEST NEWSPAPER   FRIDAY, SEPTEMBER 24 2006

DUKE BLAMED FOR HAMMOND CRASH SHOCK

by Dily Express Staff

RELIABLE information has reached the Daily Express that the Duke of Edinburgh was personally responsible for the near fatal car crash involving BBC TV Top Gear's Richard Hammond, known to millions simply as "the People's Presenter".

As hordes of grieving fans left a sea of flowers and tributes to the almost late Hammond, a top-level motoring source told us, "It was the fuggin' Duke of fuggin' Edinburgh working with fuggin' MI5 take my word for it I know what I'm fuggin' talkin' about."

As huge crowds kept vigil around the country, another source (not at all the same one) said, "There was a fuggin' white Fiat Uno which skidded into the fuggin' jet car and guess who was driving the fuggin' Fiat – the fuggin' Duke."

On Other Pages ● Why hasn't the Queen made a statement about Hammond? Show us you care, Ma'am 3 ● Was Hammond pregnant? Shock new claim 4 ● Memorial fountain to be built and then closed immediately because it doesn't work 94

THIS WEEK ON TOP GEAR WE TEST DRIVE A HEARSE...

New from Royal Mail

A special commemorative set of stamps to celebrate British achievement in the field of closing sub-post offices.

● Cotswolds: Chipping Neasden

● Black Country: Neasden-under-Lyme

● Scotland: Lochneasden

● Wales: Llanfairpwllneasden

If you want to buy this unique collection of stamps, you can't, because we've closed down your post office.

14

Duchess of Love

by DAME SYLVIE KRIN, author of *La Dame Aux Camillas*, *Heir of Sorrows*, and *Born To Be Queen Consort*.

THE STORY SO FAR: Charles and Camilla are going on a groundbreaking visit to Pakistan.

Now read on...

MR President, honoured guests, would you please welcome from the United Kingdom, His Royal Royalness King Charles and his lovely bride the Duchess of Marlborough."

The turbanned and moustachioed " Master of Ceremonies clapped his hands, as the band of the 21st Lahore Lancers struck up with "Happy Birthday To You".

A beaming Prince Charles, dressed in a short-sleeved, lightweight, tropical safari suit specially made for his visit by Roger Moore's of Savile Row, entered at the top of the ornate marble staircase of the Presidential Palace ballroom.

Camilla, by his side, was basking in the warm and sustained round of applause that greeted the Royal couple's arrival. The whole of Pakistan's high society was there in front of them. Wasn't that the Imran of Khan, the well-known former husband of Jemima Goldsmith?

Camilla didn't recognise any of the others, although she was sure that they were all very famous and important – the cream of the country's elite in fact, all turned out in their finest, just for Charles and her.

It was a far cry from the days when she had to be smuggled into the back entrance of Highgrove, hidden under a smelly dog blanket in a Sudoku 4x4.

As they descended the great stairway, like tiny figures on a giant wedding cake, Camilla felt every eye in the room was on her.

How glad she was that she had decided to wear a version of the traditional ceremonial dress of her hosts, the shimmering white and gold *shalimar kamikaze*, designed for her by the lady owner of Country Casuals in Tetbury.

The President of Pakistan himself, His Excellency General Mustapha Moustacha, stepped forward with a low bow to greet the couple and led them to their seats on the top table.

The President introduced Camilla to her distinguished table companions: "Princess Camilla, may I present to you the Shoaib of Akhtar, the Akond of Swatch and Air Chief Marshal Mohammed Ahmedgeddon, who is in charge of our nuclear strike capability, and who also has the largest collection of Elvis records in the whole of Islamabad!"

Camilla was on cloud nine and also a little peckish. She had had nothing to eat since the bag of Duchy Organic pretzels they'd been served on the Royal Flight that morning.

Almost as if her hosts were reading her mind, the dapper Master of Ceremonies clapped his hands again to proclaim the arrival of the food.

"Your Royal Majesties, Mr President, distinguished generals, I have great honour to announce that, in honour of our honourable guests, we are tonight serving the most famous of all traditional British dishes... chicken tikka massala!"

The audience clapped and cheered at the thought of the exotic culinary treat that awaited them.

Who in the world had not heard of the celebrated British love of this remarkable concoction, served in its familiar silver tin-foil cartons, accompanied by an elegant can of English-brewed Cobra lager...

AS THE waiters cleared the last of the coffee and served the alcohol-free Islamic brandy, Charles rose eagerly to his feet.

This was to be possibly the most important speech he had ever made.

For once he felt that he was standing at the very centre of world politics.

This wasn't just the usual routine Royal flimmery-flummery. This was the real thingie.

As the world divided between the West and Islam, he was the only figure on the global stage who could sort of bridge the gap.

"East is east, and west is, you know, west," he began. "But how untrue that is, when you think about it. In fact it really is appalling that anyone could say such a thing in this day and age..."

AS THE palace clock chimed midnight on the celebrated set of 24 bells cast by Fothergill & Sons of Dewsbury in 1911 to mark the Durbar of his great-grandfather King George V, Charles came to the closing passage of his lengthy but impassioned plea for peace and reconciliation between the two great world faiths.

"And that is why," he ended, "I am going to make this very important symbolic gesture by visiting one of these madrassa thingies, which are so misunderstood in the West.

"I mean, some of us know that they are centres of spiritual learning. But a great many people see them only as hotbeds of fanatical extremist Islamic terrorism, which need to be rooted out and destroyed."

At these last words, the guest on the prince's right, a highly-decorated general in dark glasses, carrying a ceremonial Kalashnikov assault rifle to symbolise his role as Head of Internal Security, jerked awake, looked worried and began talking quietly and urgently into his mobile phone...

THE morning sun was already scorching through the mosquito nets around the four-poster bed, originally built by Mitchell & Webb of Harrogate to mark the Coronation of Charles's grandfather King George VI, as Charles and Camilla woke in the guest suite of the presidential palace.

How different this all was, Charles thought, from his last visit with Diana all those years ago, when all they could talk about was what his wife was wearing.

No, this time it was about him, and the hugely important role he could play in world politics as the Defender of World Faiths – "Defensor Fidelio", as he planned to be proclaimed at his own coronation.

There was a discreet knock at the door and a smiling servant entered, bearing a freshly-ironed copy of the Lahore Daily Telegraph.

Charles eagerly snatched the paper to see how his speech had been presented.

"The Prince of Peace" was the kind of thing they would probably do, he thought. A bit over the top, but not without a grain of truth.

But what was this? A great big picture of Camilla with the huge headline "She's wearing the same dress as Di did ten years ago".

Charles feverishly searched through the paper, only to find more pictures of Camilla and Diana on almost every page.

But where was his speech? The servant came to his rescue. "The general has asked me to alert you, sir, to the item on page 94, which shows that your concerns about these madrassas have been very much addressed."

He gave Charles a wink and pointed to a small piece below the crossword.

"Madrassa bombed to smithereens – hotbed of fanatical extremist terrorism is eliminated – Royal visit cancelled."

Charles sank back on the pillows in horrified disbelief. His dejection was interrupted by the cheerful tones of the servant who was holding out a silver tray covered in a white linen cloth.

"Your breakfast, sir... it's chicken tikka massala..."

To be continued.

BRITONS SET NEW RECORD

by Our Sport Staff **Lunchtime O' Verbudget**

BRITONS today claimed a new set of Olympic records as they went faster, longer and higher than any other nation in Olympic history.

Here are the British team's extraordinary results:

- **Fastest exit of an Olympic project manager, Jack Lemley (USA), in an astonishing 7½ months!**
- **Longest building delays predicted (1.7 years!) since records began.**
- **Higher construction costs than ever before – reaching a breathtaking £5bn!**

Said a spokesman for the team, "It makes you proud to be British. This is something that this nation excels in. The Greeks may have invented Olympic building delays but we have picked up the baton and run with it – unlike the athletes who won't have a stadium, a transport system or any accommodation."

However, government spokesman Seb Coe said, "Mark my words, the 2014 Olympics will be absolutely on time."

"This is an architectural model of how it'll look"

Your Guide To Those Royal Medals

1 Order of St Smirnoff (Third Class), awarded by President Yeltsin for services to Anglo-Russian understanding.

2 Grand Star of Abu Dhabi, awarded by the Emir of Kashoggi for services to the armaments industry.

3 Croce d'Oro di Real Madrid, awarded by King Alfonso XI in a swap for the Grand Victorian Order of the Bath.

4 Congressional Medal for Supreme Valor, awarded by President Nixon during the Indo-China campaign, 1968-1975.

5 Silver Medal for Benelux Organic Biscuit of the Year, 1997, awarded by La Societé de Biscuits Organiques, Limoges.

6 Runners-up medal, Fray Bentos Anglo-Argentine Polo Championship, 1985, awarded by General Fascisto di Bastardi.

7 The Quentin Quinlan Gold Medal for Community Architecture, awarded 1999 for the design of Poundbury village.

8 The Princes Trust Medal, for Best Prince Running a Trust, awarded by the Prince of Wales, 2005

9 The Crescent Moon and Star (Tehran), awarded by Imam Ahmedgeddon for services to Inter-Faith Dialogue.

10 The Queen Elizabeth II Cross for waiting around to be King, awarded by Her Majesty the Queen, 2003, to keep him quiet.

Charles pictured here in the uniform of Grand Air Marshal of the Fleet, Chief Admiral of the Royal Cycle Corps, Ruler of the Seven Seas, Master and Commandeer **(cont'd p.94.)**

DAILY TELEGRAPH | Friday, 24 November 2006

Letters *to the Editor*

The C-Charge Debate

SIR – Once again, London's so-called Mayor, Mr Livingstone, has demonstrated his juvenile left-wing agenda by proposing a punitive daily tax on those of us whose lifestyle requires us to drive an off-road four-wheel drive vehicle around the difficult and hazardous terrain of Sloane Square and its environs. How typical of this friend of Communist dictator Hugo Chavez (not to mention Fidel Castro and Josef Stalin) that he wishes to eradicate all London's wealth-creating class just as he did the pigeons of Trafalgar Square who were cruelly mown down in a genocidal holocaust.

Sir Neville Gassington-Guzzler
1 Eton College Square, London SW4 X4.

SIR – Shouldn't the Mayor's disingenuous new proposal be called the **"con"**-gestion charge?

Mike Giggler
Via email.

The Guardian Friday November 24 2006

Letters and emails

Debate Over The C-Charge

I would like to congratulate London's Mayor, Ken Livingstone, for his brave and imaginative decision to impose a £25-a-day congestion charge on all these sickening and totally polluting, gas-guzzling, planet-destroying Chelsea Tractors, driven by stupid, toffee-nosed women whom I hate. Thanks, Ken, from all of us real Londoners who can't afford a car and wouldn't drive one even if we could, er...

Steve Spartson
Lecturer in Environmental Transport Studies, University of Hackney (formerly the Bus Ticket Museum).

Shouldn't the Mayor's amusing new proposal be called the con-"jest"-ion charge?

Mike Giggler
Via email.

FIRST EVER STATE FUNERAL FOR HORSE

BY OUR COURT STAFF LUNCHTIME O'GLUES

MILLIONS lined the streets of London yesterday to pay their last respects to the horse they knew simply as 'Dessie'.

Desert Orchid, to give him his full title, was the horse which kept the nation going during the dark days of the 1980s and 1990s.

As the massive gun carriage moved slowly down the Mall towards his final resting place in Westminster Abbey's 'Knacker's Corner', between Sir John Betjeman and Edward the Confessor, punters wept openly at their tragic loss.

Her Majesty the Queen laid a special wreath of orchids on behalf of the entire nation, as the band of the Horse Guards sounded the Last Winning Post.

Flags flew at half mast, as the capital came to a halt for Londoners to observe a two-minute silence in honour of the passing of the most iconic animal in Britain's history.

Giving the eulogy, a visibly moved Tony Blair, clutching the traditional onion, told the congregation, "He won all our hearts, we will never be the same again."

"Truly," said the prime minister, "he was the People's Horse."

A Spin Doctor Writes

MANY of us at some time or other suffer from this debilitating illness, *Feeling Fuckingus Shitus,* to give it its full medical name. Even I myself got very depressed at the prospect of losing my job and being found guilty of hounding Dr Kelly to death. Such things can of course be very lowering.

But there is a remedy and I recommend getting a High Court Judge to exonerate you and blame the BBC instead.

In my case the depression lifted at once and I was able to get on with the rest of my life. Unlike Dr Kelly who was dead.

© A Spin Doctor

School news

St Chapatis (formerly St Cakes): independent single-sex faith school, Tunbridge Wells

Jihad Term begins today. There are six boys in the school and no girls. A.L. Qaeda (Beards) is Head of Rucksacks. O.B. Laden (Caves) is Keeper of the Explosives. The chaplain, the Reverend Abu Hamza, is currently taking a sabbatical at H.M.P. Belmarsh. There will be a showing of Martyrdom Videos in the Founder's Hall on 3 October (parents welcome). Tickets from the Bursar, Abu al Achmed Mustafa Islam (formerly Wing-Commander V.J. Fenton-Snellgrove). The CCF (Combined Cadet Fanatics) will be inspected on Field Day by President Ahmageddon of Iran. The School Raids will take place on 3 September, when we welcome to the school Chief Inspector K.O.T.Y. Knacker (O.C.) of the Anti-Terror Squad, who will address pupils on the theme of "Your right to remain silent". Suicides will be on 5 November.

'MY HUSBAND WAS MONSTER'
Claims Lady Maccabeth

by Our Media Staff Jane Thane

Mull of Kintyre, Tuesday

The world of Scottish royalty was rocked to its foundations when Lady Maccabeth filed for divorce from her husband on the grounds of "unreasonable behaviour".

Said Lady Maccabeth, "Not only did he hang around with wtiches, but he had a violent streak which erupted when he murdered King Duncan and his old friend Banquo. He drank too many witches' brews and imagined he was seeing daggers in the air."

She continued, "On one occasion he was so stoned on mind-altering potions that he told me he could see a whole forest moving from Birnam Wood to Dunsinane.

"My demands are very reasonable. I want Cawdor, Glamis, half the Kingdom of Scotland and all the royalties to the song 'Yesterday, all my hubble bubble, toil and troubles seemed so far away'."

Blasted Heather

Friends of Maccabeth, however, claim that it was Lady Maccabeth who was the monster. Said one, "She is a hugely ambitious woman who will stop at nothing to be Queen.

"She lives in a fantasy world," he continued, "in which she imagines her hands are covered in blood and she can't wash it off."

A spokesman for the witches said, "We can see into the future and we can predict that the couple's lawyers will become hugely rich hereafter."

CHILDREN IN NEED
Newsreaders To Dress Up As Newsreaders

by our TV Staff **Pudsey Bore**

IN AN hilarious new send up of themselves, members of the BBC news team are to don outfits and read the news.

"It's a far cry from their usual image." said a spokesman, "We're used to seeing the likes of Jeremy Bowen dressed up as a Bond villain or Andrew Marr in fishnet tights.

"But we wanted to give viewers something out of the ordinary," he continued, "so we came up with this madcap idea of Natasha Kaplinsky and co. delivering the day's headlines wearing suits and smart dresses.

"Obviously they were a bit nervous about making fools of themselves but in the end they loved it."

He concluded, "After all it is what the BBC's for!"

"I've had so much more spare time since I decked over the houseplants"

K.J.Lamb

17

GLOBAL WARMING MEANS END OF WORLD AND POSSIBLE HOUSE PRICE COLLAPSE

By **Lunchtime O'Pocalypse**
Environment Reporter

A GOVERNMENT report, hailed by Tony Bair as "the most important document ever published in the history of the world", predicts a terrifying scenario for mankind in the very near future.

As temperatures soar to levels which will make all life unsustainable, and sea levels rise by an estimated 120 feet, flooding more than 90 percent of the earth's land mass, experts have told the Mail that house prices in the southeast of England may collapse by as much as 20 percent.

Shock

This catastrophic end of the world scenario could mean that a typical 4-bedroom detached family house in Godalming could see as much as £75,000 wiped off its asking price, overnight.

Said Sidney Greenslade, 71, a retired accountant, who lives with his wife Pearl, 69, in Chertsey, Surrey, "we bought our executive bungalow in 1987 as our pension scheme."

Horror

"Now we find that the sun is about to fry the earth to a crisp, and where does that leave me and Mrs Greenslade? I blame the government."

And the story was the same throughout Great Britain, as hardpressed, decent, hardworking homeowners read through the 565-page Stern report with a sense of mounting despair.

First-time buyers wept openly in the streets as the government report condemned them to death by drowning as the ice caps melt before they had even got a first foot on the property ladder.

© *Dacretras Productions, Kneejerk House, W8.*

Standards of grammar today really are appalling – and I'm constantly amazed at how much less clever people are than me. Take, for example, the use of the word "less" when the correct term is "fewer" – and you can see this elementary mistake, as in "6 items or less", in supermarkets up and down the country (presumably run by people who aren't clever enough to write for the *Times*!).

But I was surprised to find exactly the same mistake in hundreds of letters sent to the editor of this newspaper demanding that he print "less" articles by Mary Ann Bighead. I told the editor that the word they should have used was of course "fewer". He disagreed, and said the correct word was "none". Which just goes to show that men aren't as clever as women, and women aren't as clever as me!

© *Mary Ann Bighead*

MAN 'NOT SUING ANYONE'

THERE was astonishment today after it was revealed that a Mr G. Felton of Milton Keynes wasn't planning to sue anyone.

"I've decided not to take anyone to court to seek substantial damages for falling down a set of steps in the underground/being forced to go cold turkey/having a botched operation," Mr Felton told reporters. "I'm just going to get on with my life as best I can without blaming anyone else for my misfortunes."

However, it later emerged that Mr Felton is now planning to sue several newspapers for reporting that he wasn't planning to sue anyone.

DID GLOBAL WARMING KILL DIANA?

By Our Entire Staff
Con Spirazzy and **Maddie Tupp**

SCIENTISTS yesterday revealed that the Arctic winter that descended on Paris ten years ago causing Princess Diana's Mercedes to skid on ice whilst trying to avoid a polar bear driving a white Fiat Uno was actually caused by global warming on the direct orders of the Duke of Edinburgh.

Duke of Attenborough

Said one meterological expert yesterday, "A thick fug reduced visibility around fuggin' Paris because the fuggin' Duke ordered MI6 to increase fuggin' carbon emissions all over the fuggin' *(cont. every Monday)*

CAMERON VISITS DARFUR

I want to do whatever I can to help the poor people of Africa

Madonna's really let herself go, hasn't she?

We're All Going To Die Unless We Pay More Tax

1 Global warming is the greatest threat which has ever faced the human race.

2 Unless very drastic steps are taken immediately, human life as we know it will end in the next five minutes.

3 It is now an unchallenged fact that, as CO2 levels soar to unsustainable levels, scalding hot giant tsunamis will sweep across the world at millions of miles an hour, leaving a path of unprecedented devastation in their wake.

4 No form of life will be left unscathed, from the mighty elephant down to the humblest bacteria.

5 That includes the human race, who face imminent and painful extinction unless extremely drastic steps are taken by responsible governments acting in the best interests of humanity as a whole and those of future generations.

6 It is too late for mere talk. It is now the time for action – and unprecedentedly drastic action at that.

There can be no half measures.

8 There is only one possible way in which the planet can be saved from a fate too horrible to imagine.

9 Taxes will have to be raised immediately. And by quite a lot.

10 And, to be honest, Gordon's run out of money, so this end-of-the-world thing couldn't have come at a better time.

©The Very Stern Report
Commissioned by H.M. Treasury

"I sometimes wonder if we really need such a big vehicle"

EYE EXCLUSIVE

CLASH OF THE DYNASTIES

The Feud That All London Is Talking About

By Mail Feature Staff

FROM Mayfair to Park Lane there is only one subject that has everyone in its thrall.

The amazing bust-up that is rocking the most powerful and influential family at the pinnacle of aristocratic London society.

At the centre of the tangled web of power and intrigue stands the beautiful, statuesque Lady Annabel Fishpaste-Burlington, daughter of the 3rd Earl of Blackberry and formerly married to both multi-billionaire Sir Jammy Fishpaste, the Marmite - to - EU - referendums magnate, and Old Etonian nightclub owner Sir Mark Burlington-Bertie, well-known as the proud owner of the finest collection of handmade suits in Europe, although now, sadly, confined to a wheelchair, which has not however stopped him falling out with his son Robin Burlington-Bertie, the close friend of Greek multi-millionaire and Spectator columnist Taki Takalotof-

cokupthenos, who recently made public the split between Mark's sister China Burlington-Bertie, the Rothschild heiress, whose first cousin was once married to Zac Fishpaste, the ecologist son of multi-billionaire Sir Jams Windfarm by his fourth wife Scheherazade de Loonitoons, and top adviser on green issues to fast and rising Tory leader David 'Dave' Cameron, who is of course married to Samantha Sheffield-Wednesday, the daughter of Lord Wednesday of Sheffield. *(Keep going – Ed.)*

It was last August on a yacht moored off the idyllic Greek island of Siphylis that Sir Mark intimated that he was unhappy with the way his son Robin was managing the fashionable Berkeley Square nightspot Blunkett's, named after a previous lover of the previous wife of someone or other in his interminably boring story about some rich and rather unpleasant people who (cont'd p.94.)

RADICAL SOLUTION TO OLYMPIC BUDGET CRISIS

by Our Construction Staff **Bobski The Builder**

AS THE bill for the Olympics threatens to soar above £5bn, the government has come up with an exciting new plan to keep the costs down whilst ensuring that the project is delivered on time.

The scheme involves constructing the Olympic stadium, the velodrome and the athletes' village from a new type of building material.

Said Lord Coe, chairman of the Olympic committee, "Instead of bricks we are going to use

unsold copies of David Blunkett's memoirs.

"They are heavier than breezeblocks, denser than reinforced concrete and more impenetrable than sold steel."

He continued, "There are literally millions of these handy building components available just lying around unused all over the country and they cost almost nothing.

"The Olympic project is back on track – a track made out of Chapter 17 ('I Was Right And Everyone Else Wasn't')."

POETRY CORNER

In Memoriam Frankie Laine, popular singer

So. Farewell
Then Frankie
Laine.

Famous for many
Hits, including
I Believe, *High
Noon*, *Rawhide* and
*Champion The Wonder
Horse*.

But Keith's
Mum says that
Her favourite
Was *Ghost Riders
In The Sky*.

And now
You've become
One of them.

All together now –
Yippee-yi-o
Yippie-yi-ay...

        E.J. Thribb (78 rpm)

Lines On The Award Of The MBE To Former *Dad's Army* Star Bill Pertwee

So. Congratulations
Bill Pertwee.

You played
The Air Raid
Warden
In *Dad's
Army*.

"Put that
Light out!"

That was
Your catchphrase.

But yours
Remains
Brighter
Than ever.

E.J. 'Stupid Boy' Thribb (17½)

William Franklyn, actor and voice of the Schweppes tonic water commercial.

Schhh. Farewell then
You know who.

        E.J. Thribb
      (Scheventeen and ½)

FIRST DRAFTS

Oscar Wilde

Mary Shelley

Marcel Proust

Laurie Lee

In Memoriam Glenn Ford, star of a thousand Hollywood westerns

So. Farewell then
Glenn Ford.

You were in a great
Many films
But none of them had
Famous theme music –

Unlike *The
Magnificent Seven*
Which you were
Not in.

(All together now –
Dum Di-da-da-dum
Dum Di-da-da-dum
Da-da
Di-da-DA-da...)

        E.J. Thribb (17½)

Lines on the 50th Anniversary of the European Union

So. The EU
Is 50 years
Old.

All together
Now –

Happy birthday
To EU.

Happy birthday
To EU.

Happy birthday
Dear EU.

Happy birthday
To EU.

Sadly, however, not
Everyone
Wants to join
In.

        E.U. Thribb (17½)

In Memoriam Sheridan Morley, theatre critic

So. Farewell
Then Sheridan
Morley, celebrated
Theatre critic.

You were famous
For falling
Asleep
In the middle of
Plays you were
Reviewing.

Now you have
Fallen asleep
Forever.

        E.J. Thribb (17½)

POLICE LOG

Neasden Central Police Station

0831 hrs Emergency call received from a team of Neasden Council's recycling coordination officers (formerly binmen) operating in Milliband Lane, to report the sighting of an item of newsprint (eg, a page of the Daily Mail) which had been wrongly allocated to the green-and-yellow plastic bin reserved for bottles and jars. Six armed officers were sent to the crime scene to arrest the householder, a Mr Stephen Glovejoy, who under caution attempted to deny the offence, claiming that the newspaper must have been blown by the wind from a neighbour's blue-and-brown paper recycling bin. It was further alleged by the recycling officers that Mr Glovejoy had placed his bins on the kerbside in the wrong position, causing a possible health and safety hazard under the Placing Of Bins On The Kerbside (Health and Safety) Regulations 2006, and furthermore that he had done so a good hour and 30 minutes before the allotted "threshold time". Mr Glovejoy at this point became abusive, and the officers were forced to restrain him by shooting him seven times in the head. On return to the station, the officers were congratulated by Chief Inspector Kevin Paddington on their prompt action and bravery beyond the call of their performance targets.

1015 hrs Officers adjourned for well-deserved Full Multi-Ethnic Breakfast (formerly Full English), containing fried egg and halal bacon (not Danish), Afro-Caribbean pudding and Hot-Crescent Buns. During this time, a message was received on the station answering machine (operates 24/7 except Mondays, Tuesdays and weekends). A member of the public at Willesden West Underground Sation had observed a gang of youths of Somali appearance, "steaming" through the station with knives and causing a number of alleged fatalities and rape incidents. Unfortunately, the message was received too late for any action to be taken, although efforts are being made to trace the caller, so that she could be prosecuted for racist stereotyping of the London African community and wasting police time.

1230 hrs A number of PCs and WPCs were detailed to take all available transport to Hibbert's "The Pet People" in Mary Seacole Road (formerly Wilberforce Drive) to inspect and purchase a number of officially-approved muzzles for the station's resident Alsatian dogs, Heffer and Littlejohn. This was in accordance with new Home Office guidelines which state that, to protect the human rights of criminal suspects, police dogs may only be deployed if they are fitted with a Type 40a Canine Jaw Restraint. The station dog handlers, PCs Perivale and Queensway, fitted the appliances to Heffer and Littlejohn respectively and were satisfied that the dogs were now incapable of inflicting any personal bodily injury which might lead to a civil prosecution or compensation claim.

1400 – 2000 hrs Station closed to allow for the refurbishment of our two detention cells to accommodate 158 convicted criminals under the Home Office's new "Operation Fit For Purpose".

2132 hrs Report received from Community Support Officer Camilla Batmanjellybean that a large number of "thermostatically impaired" youths had been observed wandering round the Michael Meacher Community Arts And Leisure Complex (formerly Neasden High Street), wearing hoods, drinking alcohol from cans and inhaling hallucinatory substances. A number of members of the public had been threatened. On the instructions of Inspector Roger Fenchurch, 42 officers were dispatched to the scene equipped with bottles of water, both still and gently carbonated, to hand out to the deprived youngsters as a symbol of society's respect for their plight. A number of elderly bystanders were then arrested under The Counter-Terrorism Act 2006 for uttering inflammatory remarks about police handling of the incident. The officers involved then retired to celebrate this successful operation at the Ferret and iPod Public House (formerly the Admiral Nelson) which has recently been granted a 24-hour licence, which enabled the officers to continue their surveillance of the youths until 0430 hrs. All officers commented on the "relaxed, continental cafe-style culture" which now prevails in inner-city Neasden.

THAT CHURCH OF SCIENTOLOGY WEDDING SERVICE IN FULL
What You Missed

The Chief Thetan, Dwight J. Nutzberger III *(for it is he)*: We are gathered together to celebrate the inter-stellar union of N and M *(here he may say 'Tom and Katie' or 'Tom and Tom's next wife')*. In the name of our founder, L. Ron Hubbard, may the ceremony commence.

(Here a suitable anthem shall be played, namely the theme tune from Battlestar Galactica*)*

Chief Thetan: Do you, Tom, promise to give us all your money as long as you shall live?

Tom: I do.

Chief Thetan: Do you, Katie, solemnly swear that you have come from another planet?

Katie: Humx Da Zungl Splob!

(American translation "Indeedy, doody!" from the original Zyrgon)

Chief Thetan: I now pronounce you Level Seven Astro souls.

(There is then a collection in which the congregation hand over all their money to uniformed cybermen)

Chief Thetan: We lift up our wallets.

All: We lift them up to L. Ron!

The Recessional

The theme tune from Mission Impossible Three may be played, as the Bride and Groom depart in a spaceship for a fortnight's honeymoon on fashionable Krypton.

GUEST LIST IN FULL

Lady Poshella Beckham-Spice
Ms J-Lo
Mr Will Smith and the Men in Black
Mr John Travolta (via ectoplasm)
Mr Buzzwell Lightyear
Sir Chewbacca of That Wookey
Mr Flash Gordon (O.M.)
Ming The Useless
The Klangers

Apologies

Mr E.T., who was unable to attend as he had to go home.

Critics complain at product placement in new Bond film

by our Film Staff **Plenty O'Loot**

THE OPENING of "Casino Royale" was overshadowed this week by complaints about the blatant product placement in the new movie, which features plugs for watches, cars and computers.

But critics have been most exercised by the new infamous love scene which they claim was marred by the clumsy insertion of advertorial consumer promotion.

THAT SCENE IN FULL

Scene 94

(In the bedroom of Royale Casino Hotel. Night. Bond girl is naked in huge bed under silk sheet.)

Bond: The name's Bond. James Bond.

Bond Girl: The name's Girl. Bond Girl.

(Pause) Won't you join me, Mr Bond?

Bond: Not so fast, Bond Girl. First I have to use this ingenious gadget.

Bond Girl: What is it?

Bond: It's a Gnomeby Trouser Press.

Bond Girl: Gnomeby? They're the First Name in Trouser Pressing.

Bond: Yes, and I have a feeling that things are about to get *steamy*.

(Bond takes off his trousers and expertly removes creases using the Gnomeby 007 Trouser Press™.)

The producers of the film have denied placing commercial interests above the storyline. Last night they told reporters "Buy a Ford car! Now!"

NEW-LOOK QUEEN No. 94

The name's Elizabeth... Queen Elizabeth

MODERN JAMES BOND

IS THIS THE BEST PUBLICITY ABOUT A BOND FILM EVER?

PR AGENCIES have hailed the publicity surrounding the latest Bond film 'Casino Royale' as the "best yet".

"It's a real return to the stripped down, in your face, brutal no-nonsense publicity blitz that used to accompany Sean Connery's Bond films in the '60s."

BLUE PETER MANDELSON

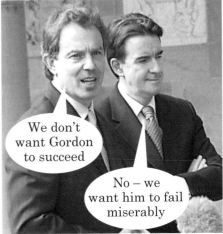

We don't want Gordon to succeed

No – we want him to fail miserably

The Alternative Rocky Horror Service Book
(as now incorporated into Common-or-Garden Worship)

No. 94 A Service of Remembrance for the Fact That We Live Today in a Multi-cultural Society

The President *(for it is she)***:** We are gathered together here today to forget whatever it is that we used to remember in less enlightened times.

All: Yeah, what was that?

President: We shall not remember all those who laid down their lives in militaristic adventures such as i.e. the First World War, the Second World War, Vietnam and all that sort of thing. I mean, they were obviously terrible events, but, you know, it hardly resonates nowadays with our modern world. I mean, we're more concerned with trying to make modern Britain a more inclusive, tolerant society of all the faiths, not just going on about people killing each other which, frankly, to my mind is totally negative.?

All: At the going down of the sun and in the morning we will not remember them.

(There shall then be played "The Last Post Office". The President shall then read out the Roll of Honour, including the names of all those who have moved into the parish in the last year)

President:

Yarosplod Poplovsky
Lukas Poplovsky
Oglot Toku
Sandor Mendic
Osambu Onanugu
Ahmed Mahmood
Mehmet Mahmood
Mahmood Mahmood
Peregrine Worsthorne

(The President shall then call for a two minute silence for everyone to meditate on how far Britain has moved on from the days when we used to make a big deal about people who had died in wars and things)

Hymn

I vow to thee my country
All earthly things above
We all live here together now
And all you need is love.

(Members of the congregation will then celebrate in their own fashion whichever festival seems most relevant: e.g. Diwali, Eid, Chinese New Year, Hallowe'en, the Winter Solstice, the December Sales.

Poppies shall then be collected and burned in the font as a symbol of forgetting whatever it is that we no longer need to remember)

WHO IS THE NUCLEAR KILLER?

continued from the front page

and the fact that Mr Litvinenko had arranged to meet the former KGB (now KFC) agent Victor Lurkov at the London Millennium Experience, Park Lane, between 12 and 12.30 am on November 2nd seems to point to a possible link with rogue Russian security elements headed by Colonel Ivan Bumpemoff and funded by the emergent Russian dissident Mafia, including exiled oligarch Boris Johnsonovich, himself a close ally of former Putin friend – turned – critic Mikhail Buggarovsky known to be in contact with Italian academic and posssible triple agent Professor Scaramouche of the University of Fandango who until recently was working on a dossier with outspoken Chechen supporting factions operating from Paris.

This all leads to one startling conclusion. We have absolutely no idea what is going on.

© *All Newspapers*

BLAIR BACKS TRIDENT

We need a nuclear weapon

You should try sushi

IS THIS THE BEST KGB SPY POISONING EVER??

CRITICS HAVE hailed the brutal, savage poisoning to death of Alexander Litvinenko as a real return to form for the KGB's "licence to kill" franchise.

"The sheer in-your-face brutality of the Litvinenko death takes us back to the classic KGB spy killings of the early sixties," said one astonished critic, "and that's why the public simply can't get enough of it."

The KGB admitted their "licence to kill" franchise had become stale and formulaic over recent years, with too much reliance on silly gadgets to kill dissidents, and that's why they had decided to go "back to basics".

"We know now that what captures the public's imagination are no-nonsense brutal murders like this."

DAILY EXPRESS

THE WORLD'S GREATEST NEWSPAPER · FRIDAY, DECEMBER 8 2006

LITVINENKO MURDER: SHOCK NEW THEORY

by Our Crime Staff Phil Page

THE MOST credible explanation yet for the murder of the dissident Russian, Alexander Litvinenko, emerged last night after top Kremlinologist Professor Fayed spoke to this newspaper.

"He was murdered by the fuggin' Duke of Edinburgh who put a white Fiat Uno in his fuggin' sushi."

Prof. Fayed then went on to say that Litvinenko was about to produce evidence that the late Diana Princess of Wales was targeted by Smersh acting on the orders of the British Royal Family who *(cont. p. 94)*

"I never watch James Bond movies... they're too far-fetched"

SUSHI BAR

My eBay

food-with-something-extra-Put-in (235)

Items I'm Bidding On (1-4 of 4 items)

	Current Price	Postage Cost	Bids
☐ **Junior Chemistry Set – 100s of fun experiments – make your friends gasp!**	£9.99	£2.99	1
☐ **Travel Guide "The Soviet Union", illustrated with 1950s views**	£4.99	£1.99	1
☐ **"Monopoly" – in dodgy state**	£2.99	£2.99	1
☐ **2 Slayer CDs, "Show No Mercy" "Reign in Blood" – a lethal dose of heavy metal!**	£9.99	£4.00	1

Items I'm Selling (1-4 of 4 items)

	Current Price	Postage Cost	Bids
☐ **"The Complete John le Carre" set of hardbacks – fair cond., some margin notes**	£15.00	£4.50	0
☐ **"Harry Potter" Official "Dobby the House-Elf" soft toy – unwanted gift**	£6.99	£4.00	0
☐ **"I ♥ Glasnost" T-shirts – all sizes, x 5m, still boxed – genuine reason for sale**	£5.00	£5m	0
☐ **"The Palladium in London" – theatre history book (bought in error)**	£4.99	£2.00	0

The Today Programme

Caroline Quinn *(for it is she)*: ...and later in the programme we shall be interviewing a number of sexworkers from the sexworker community about conditions in the sex industry. Should the government be spending more money to guarantee the health and safety of those employed in one of Britain's fastest growing service sectors?

But, first, it's Snort For The Day with the Rt. Rev. Tom Butler-Sloshed, Bishop of Neasden.

Bishop *(for it is he)*: Good evening... you know... at thish time of year... many of ush celebrating the good newsh that they've found another bottle of Irish whishkey out the back... you know... it'sh all very eashy to casht the first shtone... but which one of ush hashn't been to a party at the Irish Embassy and had a bit too much Christmas shpirit... lovely people the Irish... I love them all... one of them told me thish great joke... how did it go?... I never had a head for jokesh... anyway there wash a bishop and an actress... no, hang on, I've got that wrong... there wash jusht thish bishop... where wash I? Oh yesh, in the gutter... anyway, there he wash, being mugged... except that he washn't... he jusht made it up... anyway, none of us is perfect... which brings me to my fourth and final pint... alright, just one for the road... I mean, whatsh it all about, when you come to think about it?... Anyway, a happy Easter to you all.

J. Humphrys *(for it is he)*: Thank you, Bishop. Plenty of food for thought there!

Voice of Bishop: No, I can walk home perfectly well on my own, thank you...

(Sound of Bishop falling down BBC stairs)

Humphrys: And just a reminder that tomorrow's the Today programme will be edited by Emma Bunton, better known to some of you perhaps as 'Baby Spice'...

CHESS PUZZLE No. 94

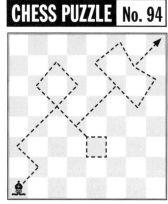

Set by Jaspistasanewto

The Irish Embassy Defence
Does the Bishop fall over before he reaches home (KR8)?

Answer: Yesh.

"Your signature, Mein Führer, it lacks authority"

Worried about being flooded this winter?

Then don't buy a box home built on a fxxxing floodplain

ENVIRONMENT AGENCY
Here to help

'RISING SEA LEVELS WON'T AFFECT BRITAIN'
Blair's Pledge

by Our Environmental Staff **Greg Dyke**

FEARS that Britain's coastline would be flooded as a result of global warming were allayed last night when the Prime Minister, Tony Blair, announced that the United Kingdom had a unique fail-safe strategy to beat the oncoming peril.

Safety Blunkett

He said, "The Environment Agency has managed to procure massive supplies of the finest water repellent material sufficient to withstand a Tsunami-style assault on our coastal defences.

"We have millions of unsold copies of David Blunkett's diaries at our disposal," he continued, "ready to turn into mile-high sea walls within days. Tests have shown that this material is totally impenetrable and is more effective than sandbags, cement, concrete or even metal barriers."

He concluded, "The Blunkett Line, as it will be known, will run from Berwick-on-Tweed in the North East, right round to Barrow-in-Furness in the North West. I would like to think that future generations will look back in gratitude to my foresight in adapting this seemingly unpromising material into a supreme environmental triumph."

New Look for Rumpole

HORACE Rumpole, the much-loved TV barrister, created in the 1970s by the world-famous playwright Sir John Nortiboys, is to be updated, in a new version more suitable for the 21st century.

Out goes the wine-bibbing, chain-smoking, overweight, poetry-quoting, politically incorrect figure who endeared himself to millions with his humorous exploits as he battled for justice in the criminal courts.

In comes the new black, female fitness fanatic, Horatia Rumbabwe, firmly teetotal and a passionate anti-smoker, who quotes the Guardian and lives with her Muslim civil partner in Hackney. The new heroine specialises in racial and gender equality cases before the European Human Rights in Strasbourg.

IPSWICH MURDERS LATEST

WILL WE OFFEND AGAIN?

NO ONE can know for certain, but psychological profilers are convinced that we will keep publishing these pictures of dead prostitutes with all the gory details again and again and again and nothing will stop us until... *(cont. p. 94)*

■ *Full story with pix (1-93)*

CAN YOU HELP THE POLICE IN THE SERIAL KILLER CASE?

By Crime Staff **Phil Pages**

WE are asking you the public to rack your brains and tell the police if you have any ideas at all about what to call the man responsible for the multiple murders around Ipswich.

So far, the Suffolk constabulary has only come up with one idea – "The Suffolk Strangler". But there are fears that this is inadequate and that officers cannot cope with the pressing demands of the media

for a suitably catchy nickname for this evil criminal.

Should it, for example, be "The Ipswich Ripper"? Or "The A14 Attacker" or "The Fat Man In The BMW"?

If you have a clue, please phone the Sun at once and we'll put it on the front page next to lovely Becky, 24, from Swindon posing in her Christmas knickers!

Yes, it's all in your super throwaway Sun!

THE SEEDY WORLD ON THE FRINGES OF SOCIETY

by Our Twilight World Staff
Janet Street-Walker

Respectable society barely acknowledges their existence and views their activities with contempt.

They have abandoned all the decencies of normal life – home, family and the values that the rest of us live by.

They are the "press workers" (the old-fashioned term "journalist" is no longer used).

They often work at night, taking money from anyone in return for their "services".

Many of them will write anything to fuel their alcohol habit and become trapped in the twilight world of the "redtop district".

A typical example of this misunderstood and frightened community is Les Filth, who would only be identified as a "reporter" on the notorious *Sun* newspaper.

"No one has a good word for us," he sobbed, in a darkened corner of Wapping in London's

seedy East End. "But there will always be a need for people like us, to write thousands of words about prostitutes and serial killers to satisfy the public's insatiable appetite for this kind of stuff.

"You may not approve of what we do," he went on defensively, "but I need the money to keep food on the table for my children and drink everywhere else for myself."

Frighteningly, not all press workers come from deprived backgrounds and broken homes.

Some of the highest-paid vice hacks come from respectable middle-class backgrounds and enjoyed the benefits of a university education. They leave their parents and families bewildered and saddened by how far their once promising children have sunk *(cont. p. 94)*

ON ALL OTHER PAGES: ● The Ipswich Ripper: A Very Long Psychological Profile by Colin Wilson **3** ● I Blame The Police by Phil Space **4** ● I Blame The Government by Phillippa Page **5** ● I Blame Men by Deirdre Spart **6** ● Why I Say The Government Should Solve The Drug Problem By Handing Out Free Heroin On The NHS by Sir Simon Junkie **7** ● "My Ipswich" by all hacks who live anywhere in East Anglia **8** ● Editors thank Suffolk Ripper for filling up dead news period pre-Christmas **94**

HESTON BLUMENTHAL'S
Cooking Made Easy Recipe Book

No. 94 The Boiled Egg

1. Build nuclear reactor and pre-heat to 4000°C.

2. Buy egg.

3. Insert egg in fissile core for 0.000073 seconds *(Tip: use atomic clock!)*.

4. Remove egg and place in liquid nitrogen tank *(Tip: at least 2000 litres works best)* to cool.

5. Remove top of egg using Laser Canon with Infra-Red Guidance System *(Tip: I get mine from the Bioweapons Department at NASA!)*.

6. Serve with toast. *(See yesterday's recipe and don't forget to use the Particle Accelerator at CERN!)*

Enjoy!

© Heston Blumensilly, The Fat Duck Restaurant, Stuffs.

"She's just seeing if the Alphabetti Spaghetti's ready"

DIARY

HAROLD
PINTER

God Rest Ye Merry, Gentlemen

God rest ye merry, gentlemen
Let nothing you dismay
Excep you've just
Had the shit blown out of you and you're
Not so fucking merry now, chums.

The Twelve Days Of Christmas

On the first day of Christmas
My true love sent to me:
A partridge in a pear tree.

On the second day of Christmas
My true love sent to me:
Two turtle doves
And a partridge in a pear tree.

On the third day of Christmas
My true love sent to me:
Three French hens,
Two turtle doves
And a partridge in a pear tree.

On the fourth day of Christmas
My true love sent to me:
Four calling birds,
Three French hens,
Two turtle doves
And a partridge in a pear tree.

On the fifth day of Christmas
I told her to fuck the fuck off
And I wanted to know what the fuck
She thought she was fucking doing
Sending me all that fucking shit.

The Little Drummer Boy

Come they told me!
pa rum pum pum pum
A new born King to see!
pa rum pum pum pum
Our finest gifts we bring!
pa rum pum pum pum
To lay before the King!
pa rum pum pum pum
rum pum pum pum
rum pum pum pum
What's that noise?
pa rum pum pum pum
Someone stop that sodding din!
pa rum pum pum pum
pa rum pum pum pum
Okay, that's it, Lady Antonia
I've had enough! Get your coat!
I can't take much fucking more of this!
We're leaving this minute!
pa rum pum pum pum
pa rum pum pum pum...

I Saw Three Ships Come Sailing By

I saw three ships come sailing by
On Christmas Day, on Christmas Day;
I saw three ships come sailing by
On Christmas Day in the morning.

And what was in those ships all three,
On Christmas Day, on Christmas Day?
And what was in those ships all three,
On Christmas Day in the morning?

What the fucking fuck do you think was
in them, then
On Christmas Day, on Christmas Day?
Bombs to blow your fucking head
off, chum.
On Christmas Day in the shitting morning.

Jingle Bells

Dashing through the snow
On a one-horse open sleigh,
Over the fields we go,
Scowling all the way;
Bells on bob-tail ring,
Making spirits sink,
O what hell it is to ride and sing
A sleighing song tonight, O!

Jingle bells, jingle bells,
Jingle all the way!
O what fucking point is there in riding
In a one-horse open sleigh
When you know you're being driven
To certain fucking death at the hands
Of George Fucking Bush and his henchman
Mister Tony Fucking Blair?

Ding Dong Merrily on High

Ding dong merrily on high,
In heav'n the bells are ringing:
Ding dong! verily the sky
Is riv'n with angels singing.
Until their wings are blown clean off
And they're shot out of the fucking sky
And plummet to their deaths.

While Shepherds Watched their Flocks By Night

While shepherds watched
Their flocks by night
All seated on the ground
They were bombed to smithereens and
That wiped the stupid grins off their faces.

As told to CRAIG BROWN

David Cameron Picks The Twelve* Top Britons In History

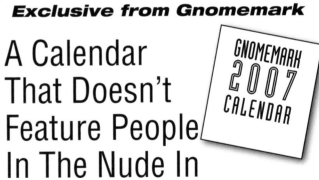

1 **Nye Bevan**, Tory founder of the National Health Service.

2 **Karl Marx**, author of *Das Kapital* and leading Conservative thinker.

3 **Polly Toynbee**, leading columnist and Tory apologist.

4 **Arthur Scargill**, legendary Tory Union leader, who led the miners strike to victory over the hated Labour Party under Margaret Thatcher.

5 **Not Winston Churchill**.

Fascist, imperialist, bow-tie wearing toff who *smoked*. Boo!

6 **Robin Hood**. He stole from the rich, gave to the poor and wore a hoodie. What more could you want?

7 **Tony Blair**. Multiple election-winning Prime Minister and role model, who courageously ditched all his party's policies in order to gain power. The greatest Tory ever.

* I know I promised 12 and only delivered 7 but I can't give you exact figures at this early stage in the electoral cycle. D.C.

House of Windsor

This Week's Best-selling Xmas Titles

1. Do Wasps Eat Fish?
2. Do Penguins Fart?
3. Are Wallcharts Crap?
4. Is Schott Shit?
5. Is Shit Crap?
6. Do Wasps Fart?
7. Are Penguins Shit?
8. Does Schott Eat Wasps?
9. Jeffrey Archer Short Stories

(That's enough books)

Letter to the Editor

Names of the year

From the Rev. Ebenezer Lockjaw.

Sir, As is customary at this time of year, I have compiled a list of the most popular names taken from your newspaper's Birth announcements:

Boys	Girls
1. Spam	Spamella
2. Ehud	Niqab
3. Panesar	Sushi
4. Polonium	Polonia
5. Ahmedinajad	Aloe Vera
6. Bond	Bondella
7. Grolsch	Stella-Artois
8. Seroxat	Herceptin
9. Desert	Orchid
10. Peregrine Wortshorne	Yasmin-Alibhai-Brown

THE REV. EBENEZER LOCKJAW, The Old Supermarket, St Anna St Airlift, Somerset.

Bruges-A-Lot!

(Palace Theatre)

NEW musical lovingly ripped-off from the wartime classic "They Flew to Bruges" (originally starring David Niven as Squadron Leader "Ginger" Squiffington and Richard Attenborough as Pilot Officer "Cowardy" Custard).

All the thrills of a night raid over occupied Belgium set to a musical comedy score that will have you tapping your toes and humming such hits as:

♪ *How do you solve a problem like Group Captain "Tubby" Trubshaw?* ♪
Somewhere over the Rhine
♪ *Sit Down you're Rocking the Lancaster* ♪
These are a Few of my Favourite Wings
Don't cry for me WAAF Sergeant Hermione "Bunty" Buntington!
...and of course, the immortal
♪ *Always Look on the Bright Side of Bruges* ♪

NIGELLA'S RECIPE FOR XMAS HUMBUG

1. Produce Xmas programme with self showing lots of cleavage, pouting, eating sausage suggestively, saying "I like it hot and steamy", etc, etc.

2. Give interviews complaining about being treated as a sex object.

3. That's it! Lovely traditional humbug!

Tomorrow: Nigella's recipe for cake. Having it <u>and</u> eating it

NEW-LOOK NAVY

MOON NOT MADE OF CHEESE – IT'S OFFICIAL!

LORD STEVENS'S LONG-AWAITED REPORT

by Our Crime Staff **Lunchtime O'Brie**

THE longest and most historic enquiry in the history of the police force came to a startling climax today when Lord Stevens of the Yard produced his verdict on the baffling mystery of the exact make-up of the Moon – it isn't cheese!

For the last five years a team of 350 officers led by Inspector Stevens has been sifting through several warehouses full of evidence in a bid to establish once and for all the truth about the Moon mystery.

Diana, Goddess of the Moon

Inspector Stevens and his men have visited seven continents, staying in some of the most luxurious hotels in the world, on their quest for the final clues that would put an end forever to the speculation that has dogged this riddle since 1997.

On a three-month visit to Cape Canaveral, they employed NASA scientists to carry out exhaustive ultra-scans, comparing Moon rock with a series of cheeses, including Lymeswold, Pont d'Alma, Althrop Blue, Gorgonblimey and the Somerset cheese Peregrine Worsthorne.

Lord Stevens himself conducted extensive interviews with top astronaut Buzz Lightyear, who was the second person ever to walk on the Moon's surface.

Mr Lightyear is believed to have told Lord Stevens that, in all his travels through space, he had never seen a white Fiat Uno anywhere in orbit round the Moon.

Furthermore he is believed to have denied categorically that Mr Neil Armstrong, his fellow astronaut, was pregnant at the time of the first Moon landing.

Lunar Tunes

Despite Lord Stevens's findings, superstore magnate Lord Fayed of Knightsbridge last night dismissed the report as yet further evidence of an Establishment cover-up, designed to suppress the truth that the Duke of Edinburgh was the so-called "Man in the Fuggin' Moon".

He was supported by the Dily Express and its billionaire proprietor, Dirty Desmoon, who pledged that his title would be giving away a million tons of genuine Moon-cheese to every reader stupid enough to buy his newspaper.

Report in full: pp 1-94.

THOSE SENSATIONAL WILLIAM PHONE TAPES IN FULL

Sensational Call Number One

Wills: Love you, Snidge.

Fruity voice: Love you too, Snooks.

Wills: You put the phone down first.

Fruity voice: No, you put it down.

(continues for several hours)

Sensational Call Number Two

Wills: Hi Bro, Rupert and Pongo are coming over and we're going to get bladdered.

Harry: Yah, good plan.

Sensational Call Number Three

Wills: So what's happening to the plonker who bugged my phone?

Lawyer: He's going to prison for a very long time.

Wills: Ha Ha Ha.

COURT CIRCULAR

Friday December 1st

Her Majesty The Queen and HRH Prince Philip will visit a Phones-4-U branch in Oxford Street where they will be introduced to the store's assistant manager, Barry.

Her Majesty will attempt to return the Nokia 3100 the grandchildren bought her for her birthday explaining that it's been nothing but trouble. However Barry will explain that her Majesty cannot receive a refund as the phone hasn't been returned in its original packaging.

Mel Gibson's **APOCALYPTO** with subtitles

Ipnopthep yukat int minotherconth*

*I blame the Jews myself

"But mostly I would like to thank God for inspiring me to write songs extolling greed, gang violence, misogyny and the sex trade..."

NEWS OF THE SCREWS

IT IS very rare in today's blame-free culture for a senior public figure to resign on a matter of principle. That is why Mr Sid Filth, the editor of my newspaper, the News of the Screws, deserves hearty commendation for his prompt resignation when he discovered that one of his staff, Mr Ken Fags, had illegally hacked into the mobile phones of members of the royal family.

Though Mr Filth had no knowledge of Mr Fags' activities, he honourably acepted full responsibility for telling him to do it and for not managing to hush it all up.

Gnome International will not tolerate its editors being caught and embarrassing their proprietor. I was therefore delighted that Mr Filth chose to resign when I told him to clear his desk and get out of the office. His place will be taken by Mr Reg Nasty, a highly respected journalist with impeccable credentials who will hopefully get some juicier royal stories than his incompetent predecessors, Messrs Filth and Fags.

> Lord Digger of Dirt,
> Screws International,
> New York-Beijing-Wapping.

MoD CLAIMS 'OUR BOYS ARE NOW READY TO FACE ANYTHING'

by Our Man In Iraq **Bazra Bombigboye**

DEFENCE Secretary Des Browne today revealed his new plan to equip every soldier in Iraq and Afghanistan with the very latest innovation in body-armour technology, guaranteed to protect them against any weapon that the insurgents are likely to use against them.

The MoD has acquired, entirely free of charge, millions of unsold copies of David Blunkett's diaries, which tests have shown provides the most effective anti-ballistic padding yet known to mankind.

Each front-line soldier is to be issued with a six-pack of the Blunkett memoirs, which he will deploy around all the vulnerable parts of his body.

Security Blunkett

Said Browne, "We are confident that the new 'Blunk-jacket', as it is already affectionately known to Tommy Atkins, will be enough to stop not just ordinary bullets but mortars, anti-tank missiles and even low-yield nuclear devices."

"But the greatest advantage of all," Mr Browne went on, "is that it is costing the UK taxpayer literally nothing at all to get this security system in place."

Lord Drayson is on holiday.

That Kate Moss/Pete Doherty Marriage Ceremony In Full

Dealer (*for it is he*): Do you, Pete Crackhead Doherty, take a great deal of drugs?

Doherty: I do.

Dealer: And do you, Kate Snorter Moss, also take a great deal of drugs?

Moss: I can't remember.

Dealer: Would the guests now like to form a line, and then put it up their noses?

Guests: Great.

On Other Pages
- Kate 'n' Pete to Divorce.

How They Are Related

Tommy Docherty	Moss Bros
Whatsup Docherty	Stirling Moss
Dixon of Docherty Green	Baroness A-Moss
Pete Bog	Anton Moss Iman
Pete Moss	Kissmee Kate
Pete Crackerty	**Cokate Moss**

A Taxi Driver writes

EVERY week a well-known Cabbie is asked to comment on an issue of topical importance. This week **Jerzy Brzgski** (minicab no. 73782567) on the problems of increased immigration from Eastern Europe.

Bloody cheek if you ask me guv this EU nonsense opening up our borders to any old Tomasz, Dickhov and Harriovski! Blimey! Coming over here in their thousands, taking all our jobs and sponging off the benefit system! My brother Lukasz, right, he's a builder and he's got 15 blokes working for him and they haven't paid a penny in tax since they got off the lorry yeah? and now these bloody Bulgarians, Romanians and what have you are trying to undercut him and put him out of business, he'll have to live off the dole innit?! Those Iraqis had the right idea I mean they should string 'em up it's the only language they understand 'cos they certainly don't understand Polish – bastards! – and as for West Ham I don't know why I support them six bloody nil they need a few Bulgarians if you ask me. I had half a dozen of those Albanians in the boot of my cab last week – very clever men... Victoria Station? Where's that when it's at home?

NEXT WEEK: Mehmet Attaturk on the need for tighter restrictions on Kurdish immigration.

Lookalikes

Borat   **Stalin**

Sir,
    There seems to be an uncanny resemblance between the controversial Kazakh investigative journalist, known and loved in the UK as Borat, and a cheery young Georgian chap, known for cunning pranks in youth (and mass murder in his mature years) and nicknamed "Koba"...

    SIAN GLAESSNER,
Via email.

Wolfowitz   **Count**

Sir,
    Has anyone else noticed the uncanny likeness between head of the World Bank Paul Wolfowitz and number-loving puppet Count von Count from Sesame Street?
    JAMES DIBLEY,
Via email.

Yeltsin   **Amis**

Sir,
    Now Boris Yeltsin's glass is half empty. Or is it Kingsley Amis?
    Yours in drink,
    OWEN MASSEY,
Oxford.

Garfunkel   **McGuinness**

Sir,
    Have any of your readers noticed the amazing resemblance between Martin McGuinness and Art Garfunkel? Could they by any chance be related? I think we should be told.
    Yours sincerely,
    SEÁN MCARDLE,

Pete   **Cherie**

Sir,
    I was struck by the remarkable resemblance between Cherie "married to an old rocker" Blair and Pete Doherty. Are they by any chance related? Would this explain the latter's musical talent?
    MATTHEW GARDINER,
Via email.

Garbage Can Man

Sir,
    I enclose a photo I took in a large store in Kentucky. I know our dear leader is looking for a new day job, but I am sure he can do better than this.   **Blair**
    TOM McGEADY,
Drumnadrochit.

Feendish   **O'Briain**

Sir,
    Has anyone else noticed the uncanny resemblance between the top contemporary comedy performer Dara O'Briain and the popular 1960's cartoon character Grimley Feendish, aka the rottenest crook in the world?
    I think we should be told.
    Best wishes,
    STEVE COWIE,
Llandudno.

Hi de Hi staff   **Beckham**

Sir,
    Has old Goldenballs Beckham been moonlighting as the Sports Instructor on a new series of "Hi de Hi" at Maplin's Holiday Camp?
    DAVID KEMP,
Luton.

Hitler   **Mugabe**

Sir,
    I find it very disturbing that the western media always portray Robert Mugabe as a vile dictator in the mold of Adolf Hitler. This can only be as a result of racial bias because in reality there is clearly no similarity between the two.
    Regards,
    MARTIN WELLARD,
Via email.

Condoleezza   **Klingon**

Sir,
    Has anyone noticed the startling resemblance between US Secretary of State Condoleezza Rice and a Klingon. Could they by any chance be related?
    PAMELA GUYATT
Via email.

Albert Steptoe   **Bruce Forsyth**

Sir,
    Are they perhaps related?
    JOHN QUICK
Via email.

Greene   **Cook**

Sir,
    I was recently struck by the remarkable resemblance between the young Graham Greene, undisputed master of miserabilist fiction, and the popular contemporary DJ, Norman 'Fatboy Slim' Cook.
    Is there something we aren't being told?
    Yours halfway between
    the gutter and the stars,
    P. GORE,
Hemel Hempstead.

Wacko   **Amiel**

Sir,

I have noticed a remarkable similarity between the somewhat eccentric songwriter/ singer Michael "Wacko Jacko' Jackson and the former newspaper scribe Barbara Amiel, now known as :Lady Black. Are they by any chance related? Brother and sister, perhaps?

Yours faithfully,
STEPHEN BRIGGS,
Litlington, Herts.

Sir Les   **Lord Levy**

Dalai Lama   **Heaney**

 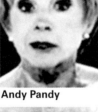

Robinson   **Andy Pandy**

Cupid Stunt   **Brand**

Sir,

Have any of your readers noticed the resemblance between Lord Levy and Sir Les Patterson, Seamus Heaney and the Dalai Lama, Anne Robinson and Andy Pandy, Russell Brand and Cupid Stunt? I wonder if, by any chance, any of them are related?

TOM CHOLMONDELEY/
JAGO TENNANT/STEVE RENDLE/
ROGER FULTON,

Via email.

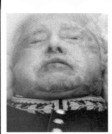 

Jabba the Hut   **Pinochet**

Sir,

Has anyone noticed the startling resemblance between the late greedy slimy malevolent and unlamented presence feared throughout the universe and the late Generalissimo of Tatooine?
JAMES ELSTON

Via email

Blair   **Jenkins**

Sir,

Have you clocked the pictures of Roger Jenkins – Britain's richest banker – in the papers recently? He's completely bald but is otherwise a replica of Tony Blair, it's uncanny.
ALAN YENTOB,

London W12.

Hogarth lady   **Ms Spears**

Sir,

Just imagine my amazement, having just returned to the UK, on discovering an uncanny likeness which may interest your readers.

Are Ms Spears and the lady in the Metro photograph related? Should we be told?
JOHN HODGE,

London W13.

Guyler   **Zoellick**

Sir,

Paul Wolfowitz may look like Count von Count (Eye 1185) but the new nomination for head of the World Bank, Robert Zoellick, is Deryck Guyler, no mistake.
DOMINIC EVANS,

Via email.

Mobutu   **Paisley**

Sir,

I wonder if there is any relationship between the Northern Ireland First Minister-in-waiting (maybe), and the dictator of Zaire? Or is it just their sense in fashion?
KAIN DARKWOLF,

Via email.

Orc   **Jackiey**

Sir,

After her intimidating behaviour in the Big Brother house, are we to assume that Jackiey Budden, the reality TV "star" and mother of Jade Goody, is the prototype of a terrifying super-race bred to take over Middle England?
I think Gandalf should be told.
ALI LISTER,

Via email.

Ray of sunshine   **Scotsman with a grievance**

Sir,

Does this picture from last week finally disprove P.G. Wodehouse's famous assertion (in 'Blandings Castle') that "it is never difficult to distinguish between a Scotsman with a grievance and a ray of sunshine"?
Yours,
ENA B. BLAIR,

London SW1.

Davros   **Murdoch**

Sir,

I could not help noticing the uncanny similarity between Davros and Rupert Murdoch. One, of course, is often considered one of the most evil beings in the known universe, while the other merely invented the Daleks. I think the Doctor should be told.

Yours etc,
ALASDAIR MCGREGOR,

POP SINGER EMBARRASSED BY BLAIRS

by Our Florida Correspondent PHIL POOL

ONE OF the world's most respected popular singers, Sir B.G. Tips, was "horrified" and "appalled" yesterday when the Eye revealed to him the decadent lifestyle of the couple he had inadvertently invited to share his Miami holiday home.

"I thought that Tony and Cherie Blair were just an ordinary prime minister and his wife," he told us. "I had no idea they were into this kind of thing."

Shock

This was the catalogue of shame with which we confronted the stunned Sir B.G.:

● Cherie has long been involved with bizarre new age cults, to which she was invited by her close friend Carole Caplin, with whom she "took showers" and engaged in Aztec "birthing rituals" while husband Tony watched.

● Tony was "turned on" by money and celebrities, and became seriously addicted to staying in rich people's houses. He had begun with mildly rich people, such as Geoffrey Robinson, but soon graduated to seriously rich figures, such as Sir Clifford Rich, and would regularly fly thousands of miles to satisfy his desperate craving for a free holiday.

● While Cherie acquired notoriety by consorting with known conmen such as Peter Fraudster, Tony was engaged in a massive scam, selling phoney peerages to scores of unsuspecting businessmen in exchange for dubious "loans". He has recently been questioned by police and could well face charges.

As we put the Eye's dossier of decadence to the iconic singer Sir B.G., he hung his head and said, "This is unbelievable. The thought of these people being in my home makes me feel physically sick.

"I can only apologise to the entire British people."

Those Tony Blair FreeBeeGees Holiday Hits in Full

♪ Stayin' A-Week ♪

♪ How Deep Is Your Pocket? ♪

♪ Knight Fever ♪

♪ Weapons Of Massachussetts ♪

(That's enough songs. Ed.)

---

theguardian

The problems of Dyslexia

More and more poeple find it hrad to matser the basics of raeding and rwiting.

A Grauniad survye revaeled that over 100 percent of its stffa are unabel to place lettres in the rihgt order. Siad one, a Mr Rubsridger:

"It is a commno preblom afflictngi middel class perants who want a good ecxuse to send theri chidlren to pravite scohols like all my staff at the Graunida." *(Cnot. p. 49)*

"Please excuse Johnny for not doing his homework, but his dog ate him..."

ENGLAND STAR OFF TO UNITED STATES

by Our Football Correspondents
Stanley Accrington and
Alexandra Crewe

THE WORLD of political football was this week left reeling at the news that ex-England captain Tony Blair has signed up to appear on the lucrative US circuit.

The future of Blair had been in doubt ever since he was dropped from the national team, and this latest move confirms that the gifted midfield schemer would not have been happy with merely a seat on the bench.

New L.A. Bore

The career of the man they call 'Loadofballs' has certainly had its ups and downs. The boy wonder who emerged in the '90s with his twisting, turning, crowd-pleasing style, forever popping up unexpectedly on the right wing, went on to enjoy huge domestic success, winning the Premiership by record points margins in 1997 and 2001, climaxing in the memorable Treble of 2005.

But recent results have been less impressive, especially in Europe, and a sleazy 'bung'

Dosh and Bucks

scandal wrecked the title hopes of many supporters. Following further humiliation after the disastrous international campaign in the WMD Cup, it was clearly time for Blair to go.

Many pundits feel that the shock move to the US has come at the insistence of Tony's wife Cherie, the former unpop performer known as Dosh. Famed for her trademark pout and love of the high life, Dosh will surely feel at home amid the glamour of L.A. and *(cont. p. 94)*

(cont. p. 94)

That New A Level Paper In Full

Politics (A level)

1. Introducing the A* grade at A Level proves that the current system is working terribly well and doesn't need changing. Discuss.

2. Recommending the Baccalauréat instead of A Levels suggests a deep commitment to the current A Level system. Do you agree?

3. Is Tony Blair's Government performing a massive U-turn on A Levels after years of talking nonsense?

  a) Yes b) Yes

Time to complete paper: Whatever

WOMAN WITH SPECIAL NEEDS GIVEN PLACE IN CABINET

by Our Education Staff **Conrad Blackboard**

A YOUNG woman, described as having "severe education difficulties", has been given a £135,000 a year place in one of Britain's most exclusive Cabinets.

The woman, Ruth Kelly (who could not be named for legal reasons), found it very difficult to learn the simplest of lessons, and could not even read the Manifesto of her own party.

When she takes up her new post, she will be given one-to-one tuition by her teacher Mr Blair, who will instruct in exactly what to say and think on all matters, until she is word perfect.

Within a year or two she will find it just as easy to explain

why she has sent her child to a private school as her colleague Mrs Harman, or even Mr Blair himself.

However, some members of the Labour Party last night expressed their fury at what they described as "unfair treatment for the elite".

Said one, "There are hundreds of people who would love the chance to be in the Cabinet – and many of them have special needs, such as a huge salary, a large car and the chance of appearing on the Today programme."

THE TIMES, Friday, December 22, 2006

Mary Ann Bighead

MODESTY FORBIDS...

It's National Modesty Week and at my daughter Intelligencia's school, St Mensa's, they ran a competition to find the girl who could come up with the cleverest slogan.

The winning entry (which I think you'll agree is very clever indeed!) was penned by an exceptionally clever girl and I knew you would want me to share it with you.

"I'm brilliant at being modest! And so is my Mum!"

Isn't that clever? I couldn't possibly reveal the name of this girl and to spare her blushes I will just refer to her as I.B.

Well done, darling!
Mary Ann Bighead.

'WE CANNOT LAST MUCH LONGER'

Moving Final Letter of Doomed Expedition Leader

by Our Saleroom Staff
Captain 'Quaker' Oates

ONE of the most moving documents of modern times is to be put on show to the public for the first time.

Dated January 2007, it is a letter from Captain Blair, leader of the ill-fated 'New Labour Expedition' which set out in May 1997 but never reached its destination.

The letter, addressed to 'whom it may concern', is written in a faltering hand, reflecting the fact that the writer knew that within a very short time it would all be over.

Here are some of the more poignant passages that the public will read for the first time.

"I fear it is all up for us. Conditions are hellish and getting worse by the day. Who would have thought that our great adventure would end up like this? From the beginning all those years ago, everything that could possibly go wrong has done so. Believe me when I say that I would have carried on if I could have done, but alas the fates have dealt me a cruel hand. You know in your heart that I have always done what I believe to be right, and I have no regrets about a single thing that I have done. I am totally convinced that everything I did since we set out was the right thing to do, and it is terribly unfair the way things have worked out. Please believe me when I say that I am proud of what we have achieved. So, God bless you all. It is getting bitterly cold. The wind is blowing at gale force. I don't think we can..."

Here the Captain's letter comes to an abrupt end. Clearly he knew that his mission would be remembered for generations to come as one of the greatest disasters in the history of the world.

WHAT WENT WRONG

May 1997. Blair expedition sets out with high hopes. Flag-waving crowds line the streets as he and his team embark on their epic journey.

June 1997. Things start to go wrong, but Blair assures his followers "Trust me, I'm a pretty straight kind of guy." They believe him.

July 1997. Team members begin to question whether the expedition is heading in the right direction. Some say they should move further to the left, others that they should move to the right. Blair insists that he knows of a hitherto unknown route, which he describes as "the third way".

August 1999. The first casualties. Petty Officer 'Mandy' Mandelson gallantly volunteered to leave the tent, but two minutes later he was back again. Blair had to ask him to leave a second time.

February 2003. More casualties. Able Seaman 'Ginger' Cook storms out in a huff, claiming that Blair is leading them in the totally wrong direction, which can only end in tears.

May 2006. 'Scotty' Brown, the purser, threatens a mutiny, claiming that he should take over. He and Blair are no longer on speaking terms.

June 2006. Blair still insists that he will carry on as leader, and that alone can bring them to their destination.

November 2006. The team belatedly discovers that Blair has indeed been leading them in wholly the wrong direction, and that for nine years they have just been going round in circles.

January 2007. Even Blair realises that the game is up and pens his moving final message to the world *(see above)*.

FOR GOD'S SAKE, LEAVE KATE ALONE!

LOOK at this picture of poor Kate Middleton! Doesn't she look harassed, unhappy and fruity? *(Surely "at the end of her tether"? Ed.)* That is why we say this hounding of our fruity *(surely "future"?)* queen must stop at once. And there's only one way to make sure that lovely Kate doesn't suffer the same fate as tragic Diana. And that's for newspapers like us to stop publishing pictures like this one. And all the others in our special 94-page supplement *'Kate – The People's Prince's Girlfriend'*.

That's why we say all responsible British publications must respect Kate's privacy – it's our patriotic fruity. *(Surely "duty"? Ed.)*

BIROS SELL OUT AS NATION GOES KATE CRAZY

by Phil Space

Kate Middleton created a fashion storm yesterday, when she was snapped holding a biro outside her Chelsea flat.

Immediately High Street stores were besieged by desperate shoppers clamouring to buy a lookalike Kate biro.

Said Colin Envelope, manager at Rymans in Haywards Heath, "I can't get enough biros to meet demand. Everyone wants to use a biro just like Kate."

Experts say that there has been nothing like it since Nigella boiled an egg using water on TV last year and everyone immediately went water mad. As a result there was a drought across the entire country as precious stocks of Nigella-style water ran out and hosepipe bans were imposed nationwide.

STOP PRESS

British pedestrians have been emulating fashion-leader Kate Middleton by walking along the pavement. "It's the in-thing for 2007," said one idiotic *(cont. p. 94)*

Early Monopoly

YES, IT'S BLUBYA BUSH
President Weeps For Latest War Casualty

by Our Man In The White House **Lunchtime O'nion**

A PLAINLY emotional President Bush yesterday failed to hold back the tears as he learnt that the war in Iraq had claimed yet another victim.

The normally cheerful Bush broke down and wept as he paid tribute to "a man who gave his political life in the service of himself".

Basil Bush

Said the late President, "The death of my career is a tragic blow to our great nation and has saddened me deeply".

Whilst the flag was lowered and the Band of the 178th Guantanamo Torture Corps struck up *'Poor George Is Dead'* (from the ex-President's favourite musical *'Oklahomaland'*), Condoleezza Rice added her tribute.

Boom! Boom!

"This is a momentous day," she said. "George Bush has become the 3000th least popular American President in history."

Dr Rice also offered her condoleezzances to the President's wife and family. Said a delighted Mrs Laura Bush, "I am still finding it hard to come to terms with the fact that poor George is not all there."

"I don't know about you, but I'm losing the will to die"

BUSH TO ACT ON 'GLOBAL WARRING'

by Our Political Climate Change Staff **Jon Snow**

THE PRESIDENT of the United States, Mr George Bush, used his televised State of the Union Address to announce his determination to act at once on the dangerous phenomenon known as 'Global Warring'.

Previously Mr Bush was not keen to admit that 'Global Warring' was taking place, preferring to talk about 'Regime Change' or the vaguer term 'Things Hotting up a Bit'.

Now, however, President Bush has acknowledge the part that the United States has played in the escalation of 'Global Warring'.

"There is only one way," said Mr Bush, "to put an end to Global Warring. And that's by invading Iran, North Korea, Lebanon, Indonesia and possibly France."

"Our target," he told the American people, "will be to go to war with at least one fifth of the planet."

THAT AMERICAN MOONBASE NAMED

New Guantanamo Bay

NEW FROM GNOMETEL

SING-A-LONGA-GORDIE

♪

I Belong To Britain
(Dear Old Britain Town)

Britain the Brave

Brits Wha' Hae ♪

Tony, Where's Yer Voters?

The Sky Plus Voting Song

♪ My Tonnie Lies Over
and Over Again ♪

Will Ye Nae Piss Off Tony Blair?

Scottish Soldier
(Regiment Disbanded)

♪ ...and many more ♪

Don't miss this Kilt 'n' Sporran Karaoke Cockle Warmer from the Voice of the Highlands himself – Wee Gordie Broon and His Band O' Renoon!

🇬🇧 That 10-point Plan for 🇬🇧 Teaching Britishness in Full

1. 'Chinese Traditional Drums' to replace 'Recorders' in all Primary school music classes.

2. Children to be taught about the slave trade in Year 9 Physics.

3. 'How the British Empire Ruined the World' to be incorporated as a module of the GCSE PE syllabus.

4. New citizenship A level: *How the Arabs invented algebra whilst British natives were living in caves unable to speak.*

5. Ur...

6. ...du

7. That's it.

This plan was compiled by top Government Britishness Advisor, Sir Kenneth Sudoku, former headmaster of the Lord Adonis Academy, Peckham.

NEW LIB DEM SEX SHAME

by Our Political Staff **Michael White-Christmas**

TOP CHEEKY Girl Ms Gabriela Irimia was today facing a storm of ridicule and derision after her decision to run off with a Liberal Democrat.

Showbiz experts predict that the Romanian singer's career may never recover from the shame of being associated with Lemsip Obit MP, the Liberal Democratic Shadow Spokesman for Asteroids.

"Gabi will have real problems being taken seriously," said one analyst. "She will be trying to deliver a sensitive song with a message, such as 'Touch My Bum', and people will just be laughing at her because of her links with Britain's third party."

Said another commentator, "It's a big mistake. She's put in all that hard work wearing tight shorts and crop-tops only to throw it all away on a man who supported Mark Oaten for the Lib Dem leadership."

He concluded, "Poor Gabi. I hope she knows what she is doing or she will become a laughing stock in the Romanian Novelty Record singing community."

TV WEATHERGIRL
Depression Coming In From Europe

You didn't predict that, did you?

7 INCHES OF HEADLINES TO PARALYSE BRITAIN

BRITAIN was put on full alert yesterday for newspapers to dump up to seven inches of hysterical headlines about snow and plunge much of the country into chaos (cont. p. 94)

COMMUTER FURY AT TRANSPORT HELL

by Our Weather Staff **Jon Snow and David Frost**

A FLURRY of trains was blamed last night for chaos on the rail network, leaving angry commuters furious at the disruption.

"We don't expect *any* trains at this time of year," said Mr Angry of Tunbridge Wells, "and under normal circumstances we would stay at home and build a snowman."

This year, however, passengers were taken by surprise when "a very thin coverage" of trains appeared on tracks around the country.

Said a spokesman for the rail network, "We had no idea there would be any trains in January.

They were not forecast and we regret that the light scattering of services that were *not* cancelled has ruined everyone's enjoyment of the winter weather.

"We can assure customers that as soon as there is any more snow – or even a touch of frost – services will return to normal and we will shut down the entire network."

ON OTHER PAGES
- Apologies cancelled again **2**
- Wrong sort of firms running the railways **3**
- Your replacement buses tonight **94**

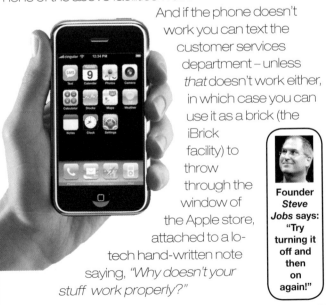

Only in the Eye

'Latin For Beginners'
by Harry Mountainsofcash

Chapter One Conjugating Verbs (*Present Tense*)

Tesco	=	I build a superstore
Tescas	=	You go shopping there
Tescat	=	He closes down his local shop
Tescamus	=	We make even more money
Tescatis	=	You feel guilty about it
Tescant	=	They can't stop us

"Of course I'm sleeping with another woman – I'm in a hospital ward!"

POLICE LOG

Neasden Central Police Station

0815 hrs Emergency call received from the former municipal swimming baths (now "Pools 'R' Us") in Hugo Chavez Avenue (formerly Ramsay Macdonald Street). The Pool Leisure Resource Co-ordinator, Ms Shelley Shellsuit, reported a very serious infringement of the Dangerous Diving Regulations 2006, implementing the EU's Watersports and Marine Pastimes Directive, 2004/45. On arrival at the facility, officers forcibly detained a Mr Reginald Pimlott, 65, who had been observed by Ms Shellsuit entering the pool headfirst by means of a diving action. It was explained to Mr Pimlott that this showed reckless disregard for the safety of all users of the pool, including himself, although at the time of the offence he was alone in the facility.

Mr Pimlott became abusive, claiming that he had been "diving in this pool since 1946". Unfortunately the accused then attempted to evade arrest, striking his head on the side of PC Stanmore's boot, thus falling into the pool and drowning. Next of kin were informed.

1023 hrs A serious incident occurred on the station premises, involving one of our recent, very welcome recruits from the ethnic community, namely WPC Niqab-Burqa. The WPC was asked to step up to receive her Grade 6 Certificate in Community Awareness Best Practice from Superintendent Pinner. When the Superintendent extended his right hand in order to shake that of the recipient, WPC Niqab-Burqa, she recoiled in understandable protest and accused the Superintendent of a deliberately inflammatory and insulting racist gesture. She explained that it was against her religion to have any physical contact with any man who was not her father, brother, uncle, grandfather or other male blood relative, as is specified in Chapter 94 of the Holy Book, the Q'ran. The Superintendent has been suspended, pending the outcome of a full enquiry into this disgraceful incident. This is to be carried out by the Islamophobic Discrimination Squad (IDS) of the Metropolitan Police, under the direction of Commander Niqab-Burqa, uncle of the victim of this horrifying attack. WPC Niqab-Burqa has been given five years' compassionate leave on full pay.

1232 hrs A report was received from a Community Support Officer, CSO Dawn Raid, who had been patrolling in the Winifred Mandela shopping precinct, when she observed what she believed might constitute an illegal item displayed in the shop window of Gameboy & Son, the Toy and Novelty Emporium ("You're Only Young Once"). No immediate action was taken by CSO Raid, but twelve hours later an armed response unit was dispatched to the premises, where they were forced to enter the shop via the front window, whereupon they seized four small packets of cards bearing the label "Happy Families".

On close examination, the cards were found to be in serious contravention of the new Gender Orientation and Sexual Equality Regulations 2006, implementing the EC's Prevention of Discrimination (Sexual Equality and Gender Orientation) directive, 2004/46.

None of the families featured in the game were same-sex partnerships of either a gay or lesbian nature – i.e. Mr Bun the Baker was married to Mrs Bun the Baker's Wife, and not to Mr Cake the Other Baker. Similarly Mrs Bun was not portrayed as the live-in civil partner of Ms Sausage, the butcher's lesbian daughter, nor were they shown as living happily with their two adopted children, Master Onanugu from Nigeria and Ms Polly Pot from Cambodia.

"The more closely we examined this game," as Sergeant Northolt noted in his report to the Crown Prosecution Service, "the more seriously we realised that it was a highly dangerous object which needed to be rendered safe immediately. Under the direction of PC Hainault of our Explosives Division, the packs of cards were destroyed in a controlled explosion, which un- fortunately razed to the ground the entire shop, including the late Mr Sidney Gameboy, the toyshop owner, Nora Gameboy, the shop owner's wife, Master Archie Gameboy, the toyshop owner's son, and Miss Jade Gameboy, the toyshop owner's daughter."

1513 hrs A series of messages was left on the station answering machine, recording various acts of murder, rape and grievous bodily harm which had been committed in the Neasden district, following the release of 317 A-Category prisoners back into the community as a result of prison overcrowding at Neaswood Scrubs High Security Open Prison. Callers were redirected to our Crime Prevention Counselling Service in Lahore, where they could listen to soothing extracts from classical music by a Mr Vivaldi until an agent was available to tell them that the police station was closed.

'RAKE' TO SUE

AN internationally famous celebrity rake today confirmed that it would be suing a newspaper over claims it had encouraged impressionable girls to aspire to be rakes.

"I've never had an eating disorder, I eat like a rake," insisted the rake *(cont. p. 94)*

"Gosh, how thrilling – what would I have seen you in?"

A Pompous Statement from Channel Four

Channel Four is firmly against the bullying of minority groups and deplores any attempt to incite hatred against any person on the grounds of who they are or where they come from particularly if the victims of this bullying are directors of national broadcasting companies. These people have an absolute right not to be abused merely because they work for Channel Four and because they happen to belong to a small group of individuals who believe that Big Brother should continue to be shown on national television. We believe that using insulting or pejorative language to describe Channel Four directors is unacceptable, particularly phrases such as 'cynical, greedy tossers' or 'cowardly, self-serving hypocrites'. Worst of all is the intimidatory call for Channel Four directors to "Go home and get someone decent to run the Channel". Such remarks are merely the result of the kind of ignorance and stupidity that are all too prevalent in a society which has been reduced to watching Big Brother.

© Channel Poor

T V PROGRAMME PLANNING —

"WHAT WE FUCKING NEED IS MORE FUCKING PROGRAMMES WHERE EVERY-FUCKING-BODY SPEAKS LIKE REAL FUCKING PEOPLE.."

That Unbroadcast Racist Big Brother 'Limerick' In Full

There once was a programme so tacky
That its contestants almost said "Paki".
But the bosses at Channel Four
Just commissioned some more
Because Big Brother got big ratings and despite their behaviour none of those responsible were given the sacky!

"We were going to have a wind turbine, but they're not very efficient"

NUCLEAR POWER STATION

■ Shh... Jade!?! We never want to hear from you again. Why don'tcha just clear off back to that gutter you should never have climbed out of in the first place, and take your old slag of a mother with you?!? Along with your half-witted apology for a boyfriend while you're at it!!?! OK, so you're educationally sub-normal, fat and ugly!?! But that doesn't give you the right to commit racist bullying on one of India's most useful leading ladies!?!! No wonder the whole world threw up as they watched you behaving like a cross between a wild pig and a member of the Gestapo!?! Frankly, it made me and millions of others ashamed to be alive!!?!

■ Shh... ut up everybody!!?! Going on about Jade Goody!!?! What's all the fuss about??! She only says what you hear in a thousand pubs every Saturday night!?!?? It's only a television show, for gawd's sake!?! What have we come to as a nation when we go all mental over a few harmless jokes and some crosswords over some overpaid curry queen from Calcutta?!? Shh... ut up, Shilpa, and shh... ove off home to poppadom land where you belong!??!

■ Shh... ameful!!! Have we got nothing better to do as a nation than sit around all day long talking about some tacky celebrity reality show?!? You wanna know about real reality, mister?!? There are people dying out there!?! Millions of them!!?! Bombs are going off!?! The ice caps are melting!?! There are huge gales blowing half the country away!?! And all the newspapers can do is drivel on about Jade and Shilpa, as if anyone knew who they were – or could care less!?! Time to wake up and smell the perfume!?! (Geddit?!)

■ Shh... irty Shilpa and Jokey Jade have done us all a favour!! So thank Gawd for Celebrity Big Brother, for taking our minds off all the horrible things going on in the world!?! The terrorists!?!! The global warming!?! The trees falling on your car!??! They've given us a good laugh and a little bit of warmth to melt the winter snow!?! *(Shurely 'a profound insight into the state of modern Britain'? Ed.)* When they start handing out the Oscars, it should be Dame Jadi, not Dame Judi, who gets "Best Actress" (geddit?!?).

■ *HERE THEY are – Glenda's Channel Four Bully Boys!!*

● **Luke Johnson,** Channel Four's chairman!?!! You can deliver your pizza round to my place any time!?! But make sure it's American Hot?!! Geddit?!?

● **Lord Puttnam,** non-executive director of Channel Four?!?? Come round to my place and I'll set your chariot on fire?!?? Geddit?!?!

● **Peter Bazelgette!?!** Crazy name, really disgusting programme!?!!

Byeeee!!!

A Taxi Driver writes

Paul Dacre (cab no. 7426324) on the "Institutional Bias of the BBC".

Blimey listen to that on the radio guv, bloody BBC letting Blair off the hook! British Broadcasting Corporation? The Blair Broadcasting Corporation I call it! Bush House? Anti-Bush House in my book! White City? Pinko City more like! The Today Programme – they should call it the Toady Programme, the way they treat Tony and his mates! And the newspapers are no better! Guardian? Independent? Times? They're all up Blair's bum, aren't they guv? Do you know what I'd do if I had my way? String 'em up! It's the only language they understand. I'll tell you what, though, have you seen the way house prices keep going up? Not everything is bad is it? Not that they'd tell you on the BBC – or Biased Bollocks Crap as I call it. Ha ha ha! I had that Richard Littlejohn in the back of my paper once. Very clever man.

NEXT WEEK: Charles Moore (The Metropolitan Hansom Cabriolet Service Number One) on why spats are making a comeback (Surely "Tories"? Ed.).

CATHOLICS IN ADOPTION ROW

"I'm a simple girl who's got herself into trouble"

"Don't look at me – it's not *my* baby"

CAMERON JOINS IN

"I'd like to adopt some gay votes"

That Honorary Degree Citation In Full

SALUTAMUS GORDONUS BROWNIUS CALEDONICUS MOROSUS ET HUMORLUS PER MULTO ANNUS CHANCELLORIUS EXCHEQUERUM NOMINE "FERRUM CHANCELLORUM" ET "AMATOR PRUDENTIAE" FAMOSUM PER SERMONES LONGISSIMOS ET ORATIONES INTERMINABILOS INCOMPREHENSIBILOSQUE DRONAVIT INSTRUCTANS POPULUM BRITANNICUM IN THEORIO NEO ENDOGENO BALLSENSIS TOTALIS. QUONDAM AMICUS ANTONINUS BLAIRUS IMPERATOR ET DUX UNIVERSUS ETCETERA SED NUNC HOSTIS IMPLACABILIS NONSPEAKUS MAXIMUS. MEMORANDUM SEMPER "CONCORDAT GRANITA" QUANDO ANTONINUS PROMISSAVIT IMPERIUM SUPREMUM AD GORDONO SED RENEGAVIT DURANTE DECEM ANNOS MISERABILIS. GAUDEAMUS GORDONUS FURIOSUS ET BITTERENSIS!!

© Newcastle University (formerly The T. Dan Smith Polytechnic, Gateshead).

The Alternative Voice

CEDRIC SPART (Co-Chair of the Tufnell Park Gays and Lesbians Alliance Against the Iraq War, Hunting and the Catholic Adoption Society).

Once again the homophobic bigots who run the Catholic Church have come out in force to blackmail the elected government of this country in its bid to end the centuries of hatred and persecution of gays and lesbians in denying them their basic human right to have children. What do these so-called Archbishops, who dress up in women's clothes and protect homosexual priests, know about gays... er... for once the government has got it right in standing up to the homophobes and making it a criminal offence not to have a gay or lesbian parent... er... this is a great day for tolerance and equality and it's time the Catholics and all the other religious bigots were silenced for once and for all, except, of course, our Muslim friends, who have every right to believe that homosexuality is a sin, so long as they don't bomb my home... er... (cont. p. 94)

The incredible new novel from legendary storyteller Judas Iscariot

The Gospel According To Jeffrey

HE IS the most hated figure in the whole of history – a byword for dishonesty, greed and perjury *(Surely 'treachery'? Ed.)*

But now author Judas turns history on its head. Drawing on new evidence provided by world-famous scholar Professor Baloney, Judas asks, "Have we got it all wrong? Was Jeffrey in fact the most saintly man who ever lived?"

Says Judas, "Jeffrey has been vilified down the ages. But in reality he was an ascetic figure, living on top of a tower by the riverside, subsisting on a diet of nothing more than shepherd's pie and champagne while he wrote his sacred texts."

Judas proves conclusively that Jeffrey married the saintly Mary, whose odour of sanctity was so fragrant that judges fell down in a swoon at her passing.

In fact, concludes Judas,

Jeffrey may well have been the Son of God, only cheated of the top job by envious scribes and Pharisees who delighted in making up malicious stories about how he spent his evenings in the company of prostitutes and tax avoiders *(Surely 'gatherers'? Ed.)*

"Worth every penny of the 30 million pieces of silver he was paid by his publishers."
Sunday Times

"Hanging is too good for him"
The late S. Hussein

"We appreciate your efforts to be religious, but there's still no room at the school"

Reid Pledges Crackdown On 'Chinese Immigrant Army'

by Our Political Staff **Terry Cotter**

THE Home Secretary, Dr John Reid, today promised to halt the threatened "invasion of Britain" by thousands of terracotta Chinese warriors.

Said Dr Reid, "Obviously we are concerned about this number of immigrant statues swamping the entire country, placing an intolerable burden on our already overstretched infrastructure, and that is why I have to take firm action."

The Home Office has laid down that the number of ethnic Chinese warriors of terracotta extraction permitted to enter Britain will not exceed 12.

Last night, however, critics were quick to point out that, since Britain no longer operates any border controls, there is nothing to stop millions of the gallant oriental warriors from entering the country by train, aircraft, boat or even from being smuggled on the back of lorries on Eurostar, all demanding to be housed in the British Museum.

▶ **Fact:** The terracotta army, consisting of 2 million identical life-size figurines, was commissioned by the legendary Emperor Lib Dem Ming during the 3rd Century BC. When the aged Lib Dem saw the warriors, he decided that they were so boring that they should be buried in a huge hole in the ground. This was rediscovered in 1974 when a peasant was attempting to dig his way to Britain where his cousin had recently opened Glasgow's first Chinese takeaway. The Emperor Ming believed he was immortal and would one day rule the world with his army of Lib Dem councillors *(Surely "terracotta bores"?)*, aided by his trusted henchman Lem Sip Opek.

Private Eye is offering readers the chance to win 2,000 free tickets to see the new exhibition. All you have to do is name three of the Lib Dem party's front bench spokesmen (not including The Cheeky Girls)

Snow White And The Magnificent Seven Dwarfs

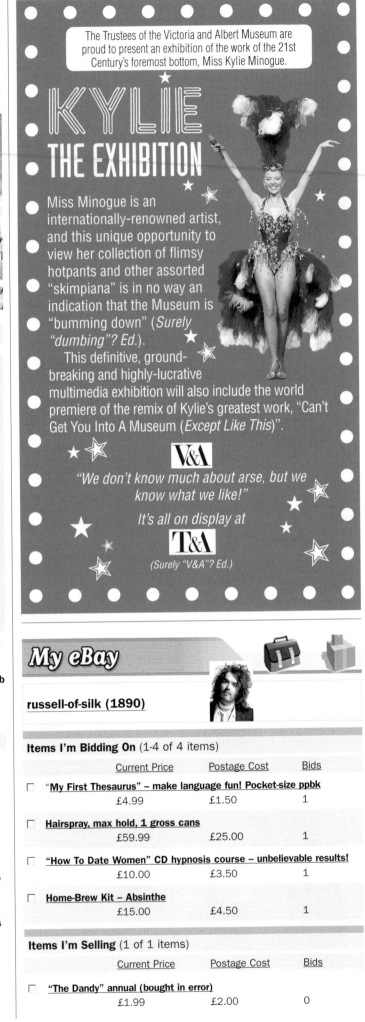
My eBay

russell-of-silk (1890)

Items I'm Bidding On (1-4 of 4 items)

	Current Price	Postage Cost	Bids
☐ **"My First Thesaurus" – make language fun! Pocket-size ppbk**			
	£4.99	£1.50	1
☐ **Hairspray, max hold, 1 gross cans**			
	£59.99	£25.00	1
☐ **"How To Date Women" CD hypnosis course – unbelievable results!**			
	£10.00	£3.50	1
☐ **Home-Brew Kit – Absinthe**			
	£15.00	£4.50	1

Items I'm Selling (1 of 1 items)

	Current Price	Postage Cost	Bids
☐ **"The Dandy" annual (bought in error)**			
	£1.99	£2.00	0

NORFOLK SKIES DARKENED AS FURNACES BURN

by **Lunchtime O'Bootiful**

PILLARS of smoke over a mile high filled the Norfolk skies today, as lorry-load after lorry-load of doomed books headed for the blazing incinerators working round the clock to destroy what they are calling "the biggest publishing turkey of all time".

Every single copy of David Blunkett's diaries *The Years of Boredom* has now been destroyed, it was later claimed.

But there are fears that even more books could still flood in from abroad when they are returned by disappointed book dealers.

● *For a full version of this story, visit www.blunkettbookdisaster.com*

● *Did you enjoy reading the above details of how to get a fuller version of the Blunkett story? Let us know at Eye Noticeboard www.getalife.com*

Beano Boris on the implications of the recent outbreak of Avian Flu

"I've always liked stuffing the odd bird"

Blimey! Johnny Foreigner has got the nerve to give the old thumbs down to honest British turkey – just because it's got some killer disease! Cripes and double cripes! Isn't that just typical of our cowardy custard cousins from abroad! Well, never fear, yours truly is going to start gobbling turkey as if there was no tomorrow!

Which there will be, by the way, whatever the scaredy-cat boffins try and tell you! Mmmm... Turkey Twizzlers, Turkey Nuggets, Turkey-flavoured Turkeys with Turkey Sauce. That's what's on the Beano Family Menu from now on. And jolly yummy tuck it is too! Anyway, I've been scoffing brother turkey for my whole life and it hasn't done me any harm! What? Atishoo! Atishoo! Yikes! Crikey! Oooo-er! Anyone know any doctor chappies?

On other pages ● Is it safe to read Boris's column? A doctor writes

FACe TRANSPLANT WARD

It's floo-tiful!

Surely Boo-tiflu?

The Today Programme

6.42 a.m.

Woman with posh voice *(Sarah Montague, for it is she)*: ... as the great bird flu pandemic reaches crisis proportions, we go over to the government's chief veterinary scientist on the spot in Suffolk.

Good morning, Mr Clipboard, you are the government's chief veterinary scientist on the spot in Suffolk.

Clipboard: Good morning.

Montague: And I think the question everyone is asking this morning is just how likely is it that this deadly strain of HN51 avian flu swill spread to the human population?

Clipboard: That is extremely unlikely.

Montague: So what you're saying is that it's now only a matter of time before this killer virus claims its first tragic human victims out here in Suffolk?

Clipboard: No, what I was saying is that such a scenario is highly unlikely.

Montague: So you agree with me that it won't be long before millions of men, women and helpless toddlers are dying a slow and painful death?

Clipboard: I think the chances of anything like that happening are so low as to be negligible.

Montague: A frightening prospect indeed! And still on the bird flu story – we're just getting some breaking news that apparently one of the poultry workers has got a nasty cough, which confirms everything that the ministry vet, Mr Clipboard, was telling us this morning.

And we're going over live now to our reporter Phil Airtime, who is standing outside the home of Dave Henpusher, the poultry worker who is almost certainly the first of millions of people in this country who are doomed to die of this terrifying plague.

Phil, what are you hearing out there on the spot in Suffolk?

Airtime: Well, Sarah, I'm standing here outside the home of Mr Henpusher, who works at the poultry plant which is at the centre of the crisis. Information is a bit sketchy at the moment, but what we do know is that Mr Henpusher didn't go to work this morning because he was suffering from a very severe cough.

I'm now looking at his bedroom window across the street, and I can tell you that the curtains are still completely drawn and that there is no sign of life.

Montague: So the chances are that he's dead? Is that the feeling where you are, Phil?

Airtime: Absolutely, Sarah. It's obviously too early to speculate, but what we are hearing is that there is every indication that the long-feared killer flu epidemic has now claimed its first British victim.

Montague: Well, we'll have to leave it there, Phil, but thank you for confirming that bird flu has claimed its first British victim. And now it's time for the latest headlines from Jim.

Jim Naughtie *(for it is he)*: And here are today's headlines. A Government scientist has dismissed fears that the Suffolk bird flu outbreak will spread to humans. And Suffolk poultry farm worker Dave Henpusher has tested negative for any sign of the virus. He has gone to the chemist to buy some cough sweets and hopes to be back at work later this morning.

And now – Thought For The Day, from our old friend, Rabbi Lionel Blue.

Rabbi Blue: Hullo Brian. Hullo Sailor. You know, we've heard a lot about global warming, but as my old granny used to say *(cont. 94kHz)*

41

Tonight's TV

Pothead Revisited

(UK Old 9pm)

ANOTHER chance to see the classic saga of bright young things living it up among the dreaming spires of Oxford. In tonight's episode gilded youth David and his inseparable companion Boris decide to trash the Golden Curry House and push an oik off Magdalen Bridge. But later they are arrested by Inspector Morse for possession of cannabis.

Eye rating: Zzzzzzz

A Doctor Writes

AS A DOCTOR, I am often asked, "Will the NHS computer transform the Health Service as we know it?"

The simple answer is GP FAULT 0847x6... bugger... how do I get out of this this this this this? Where's the number of the IT bloke? ... FATAL EXCEPTION 0D... INVALID PAGE FAULT... STOP: 0xC0000221 STATUS_IMAGE_ CHECKSUM_MISMATCH. © A. Doctor 2007.

COURT CIRCULAR

Yesterday

His Royal Highness the Prince Harry attended the official opening of a bottle of vodka at 'Slappers Niteclub' in Kensington. His Royal Highness was accompanied by Lt. 'Pongo' Ricketson-Smythe (3rd King's Own Chunderers), Lt. Charlie 'Snorter' Snortington (17/21st Royal Green Wellingtons), Miss Chelsea Tractor, Miss Fruitella Fruitington, a bloke they had met in the pub earlier who seemed like a good laugh, and some other people who he can't remember now.

The Prince was introduced to a number of cocktails including 'The Shit Face' (8 parts rum, three parts brandy, 2 parts anti-freeze), the 'Hogwhimperer' (absinthe, curacao, Windolene) and the 'Va-va-vom' (a yard of gin with a bucket of Baileys chaser).

The Prince and his party proceeded to the floor before being accompanied out of the club by Mr Dean Meathead (Fellow of the Royal Institute of Bouncers). He then attended an informal photocall in the gutter with Mr Len Scap, Mr Sid Snaps, Signor Sleazi Papparazzi, Monsieur Phil Espace and various other representatives of the international press.

Today

The Duchess Fergiana will attend the opening of a cheque book held by American Society magazine, Bizarre Harpies. She will proceed to be rude about the Royal Family and then complain that they never invite her round any more.

She will then sit for an official portrait by top American society photographer, Adobe Photoshop, accompanied by his assistant, Plenty O'Airbrush.

Tomorrow

Her Majesty the Queen Helen Mirren will receive many hundreds of awards from her loyal subjects.

On The Widening Disparity Of Income In Modern Britain

LET's face it, nowadays you are either one of the "Haves" or the "Have Lots"! Or the "Haves" and "Have Yachts"!! Or the "Haves" and "Have Noughts" after their City bonuses!!!

I'm not envious of the new super-rich with their plasma-screen helicopters and their ski chalets in Barbados, but I can't help thinking the wealth gap between decent hard-working, life-style columnists and disgusting, über-rich merchant bankers is getting out of hand!!

AS A working mum with a small toddler, I'm more of a "Have Snot" than a "Have Pots"!!! And since the Useless Simon thinks that the best way to earn a living is to slob about watching Pro-Celebrity Near Fatal Crashes with TV's Richard 'Hamster' Hammond on BBC2, there's no way *we'll* be flying off to the moon in a private jet!

Ok, I'd like hot-and-cold running staff, like some of our neighbours, rather than one useless girl from Poland who couldn't even plumb in a new boiler system! I'm not so much a "Have Got" as a "Have-Szlot" or whatever her stupid name is!!!

But don't get me wrong! I'm all for people being rewarded for their work – apart from Szlot, obviously, who is going straight back to Krakow, which will make me a Slav-not!!! But when the journalistic grafters of Britain can't afford the same sort of holidays as the ghastly vulgar people opposite us, something is rotten in the state of West London.

It's what I call the difference between the "Haves" and the "Have-Notting-Hills"!!!!

Polly Filler's best-selling new book "Punny Money", a hilarious sideways look at the British Economy, is published by Johnson & Johnson £17.99.

"Be honest, has sex become a chore?"

How many Times a week?

The biggest-ever report on our secret habits

AN extraordinary new survey reveals that the average couple is having the Times newspaper only once or twice a week. Some are having it less than once a month and 69% of the population never have the Times at all.

Other disturbing results show that men in their fifties are more likely to be unfaithful to the Times and start reading the Daily Telegraph. However, women in their thirties are most prone to fantasise about buying the Daily Mail.

Said leading sexologist Sir William Rees-Snogg, "It's clear that people's habits have changed. Many adults are just too tired to have the Times and would rather have sex than read another boring survey in the Times."

Full results, charts, suggestive pix p. 94

WHERE ARE THEY NOW – THE GLITTERING PRATS OF 1987?

The Eye follows the fortunes of David Cameron's fellow members of the most elite dining society in the history of the world, Oxford's legendary Bullshittingdon Club

1 **David 'Spliffy' Cameron,** Old Etonian, now tipped to become Britain's next prime minister. Took a First in Public Relations and Media Studies at Snortnose College.

2 **Boris 'Beano' Johnson**, Old Etonian, now tipped to become the ex-editor of the Spectator. Read Comics at Cripeschurch College.

3 **Augustus 'Gussy' Fink-Nottle**, Old Etonian, son of Lord Hitbottle, now a hedge fund manager at Fink and Nottle (this year's bonus £700 billion).

4 **Peregrine 'Perry' Starborgling**, Old Etonian, son of merchant banker Sir Arthur Starborgling. Married heiress, the Hon. Poppy Moneypenny, sister of the Hon. Penny Moneypoppy. Now works for Starborgling Securities (Riyadh).

5 **Rodney 'Dipso' Ricketson-Hatt**, Old Etonian, was President of 'the Buller' while reading the wine menu at the Randolph Hotel. Set up a dotcom business, Sockittome.com, selling thermal footwear on the internet, but now lives in Tasmania, working as a landscape gardener.

6 **Bartholomew 'Corby' Trouserpress**, Old Etonian, now a senior partner in top City law firm Trouserpress, Trouserpress, Trouserpress and Chaudhuri. Read the Daily Telegraph at Lady Margaret Thatcher Hall.

7 **Sebastian 'Pratt' Prattwinkle**, known to his fellow Bullers as 'Oik' because he went to Westminster, not Eton. Started a restaurant 'The Guzzling Toad' in Trowbridge, Wiltshire, with family money, but now faces bankruptcy proceedings. Entered the Priory, where he shared a room with Jonny Knatchbull-Trumpington (President of Bullers 1984-5) and *(That's enough Prats. Ed.)*

Andrew Neil's Desert Island Disc Choices In Full

1 **Brown Girl In The Photo** Boney M

2 **Simply The Vest** Tina Turner

3 **The Lady Is In Tramps** Frank Sinatra

4 **Sunday Bloody Sunday Times** U2

5 **St Matthew D'Ancona Passion** Johann Sebastian Bachlay-Brothers

6 **Is This The Way To I'm A Brillo?** Tony Christie

7 **Pad!** Michael Jackson

8 **Brown EYE Girl** Van Morrison *(You've done this one. Ed.)*

WIMBLEDON EQUALITY CALL

by our Wimbledon correspondent **Maria Sharapovphwoarr!**

MALE PLAYERS at Wimbledon have demanded to be on an equal footing with their female counterparts after it was revealed that women players receive substantially more pictures in the Daily Telegraph and the Mail than them.

"No matter how well we play, the front page of these paper will always be full of long-legged Russian blondes in tiny micro-skirts," complained world number one Roger Federer. "It doesn't matter if one of them gets dumped out in straight sets in the first round, they'll always receive substantially more photos than me."

The newspaper editors rejected the complaints, saying they would give an equal amount of space to the male players. Just as long as those male players were blonde, leggy, Russian and female.

A VERY INAPPROPRIATE PLACE FOR AN ANTONY GORMLEY

① ON A ZEBRA CROSSING

SIT DOWN MATE!!

② IN A CINEMA.

PHILIP WARNER

THAT ALL-PURPOSE JONNY WILKINSON PIECE IN FULL

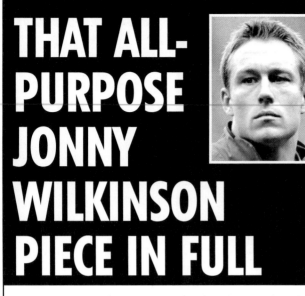

THREE CHEERS/yawns for Jonny Wilkinson, England's rugby superhero/superbore. Yes, he's the dishy/dull beefcake who makes the nation's women swoon/snooze. Can anyone think of anything more exciting/tedious than watching England's dreamboat/automoton kicking England to glory/killing the game off.

With his rippling/over-developed torso and his thunderous/freakish thighs, Wilko is the stuff of every girl's dreams/nightmares.

Good At Kicking/Needs A Good Kicking

Welcome back/clear off, Jonny. It's great to have you back, so that we can have something to be proud of/start attacking you again.

Nursery Times

············ Friday, March 2, 2007 ····················

JEMIMA AND GRUNT– IT'S ALL OVER

by Beatrix Harry Potter

YES, all the birds and the bees were a-sighing and a-sobbing when they heard the news that the farmyard's favourite couple have decided to go their separate ways.

Pig-about-town Hugh Grunt and the beautiful Jemima Puddleduck, daughter of the late Sir Jeremy Fishpaste, the marmite magnate and amateur angler, have finally split, after a stormy relationship that had long been the hottest gossip item in Nurseryland.

The Pig Issue

Friends of the couple assure me that no other farmyard animals are involved.

But, they tell me, "at the heart of it is Grunt's inability to commit and make an honest duck of Jemima".

However, Lady Annabel Puddleduck, Jemima's handsome mother and widow of Sir Jammy Dodger, the biscuits-to-jam king, told me last night "there are plenty more fish in the pond as my late husband used to say, before he was tragically swallowed by a gigantic trout".

Having a Quick Duck

Wasting no time, Grunt has hastily made it up with his ex-bunny girl, Miss Liz Flopsy, whose forthcoming wedding to the Indian elephant Mr Ali Barbar, is the talk of the jungle.

It seems that Grunt has agreed to be the Best Pig at the three-week long nuptials and to make a speech in which he has promised not to poke fun at Mr Barbar, or to make embarrassing jokes about he and Miss Flopsy being "at it like rabbits" during their many years together.

MOSLEMS LOSE FIGHT TO WEAR BOMBS ON TUBE

by Our Legal Staff
Michael Burqa and Niqab Ross

AFTER a challenge in the High Court, a 16-year-old schoolboy from Dewsbury, Yorks, was told that it was not an infringement of his human rights to be told to take off his explosive rucksack before using public transport.

The boy, Osama bin Ladenwithbombs, cannot be named for legal reasons but plans to appeal.

(Reuters)

NON-MUSLIM SPEAKS OUT

It's a police state. I'm being unfairly targeted

ISLAMIST LOGIC

Part 94

"Britain is a police state for Moslems with a judiciary and police force enforcing heavy-handed, bigoted laws..."

"... which is why we need to introduce Sharia Law as soon as possible"

CLINTON FOR PRESIDENT

I'm going to try and do what you did in the nineties

Phwoar! Can I watch?

"And this was knocked through by the last owner. It's some kind of portal..."

Russell.

GOLDSMITH 'CHANGED ADVICE' TO HIMSELF OVER 'ILLEGAL ENTRY' INTO BARRISTER

by Our Legal Staff **Joshua Rosenbeard**

THE Attorney-General, Lord Goldsmith, it was revealed last night, had "radically changed" advice given to himself on the proposed incursion into the bed of a fellow lawyer, Ms Dollis Hollis QC.

Initially, in a written opinion addressed to himself, Lord Goldsmith advised strongly against the proposed incursion of Ms Hollis's "private territory", on the grounds that it would be "wholly improper" and "entirely unjustified".

Goldsmith's opinion, marked "For My Eyes Only", went on, "Having considered the various options open to me with regard to the proposed course of action, I am strongly persuaded that it would be unethical, fraught with risk, and quite possibly might end in my wife finding out.

"For these reasons, *propter aliquod re legoverensis*, I am minded to advise my client, myself, to refrain from pursuing this affair any further."

Weapon Of Self-Destruction

Only a few days later, however, according to documents which have come to light under the Freedom of Fornication act, the Attorney-General unaccountably reversed his earlier opinion.

In an amended version, he wrote, "Why not? You only live once! Dollis is an absolute cracker, esepcially in that wig! Go for it, my son!"

The question remains – what was it that caused Britain's top legal officer to *(cont. p.94)*

HOW JOB HAS AGED BLAIR

1997

2007

"Oh dear, oh dear. What cowboy did your face transplant?"

𝕿HE 𝕭OOK OF 𝕷EVY

Chapter 94

1. There was, living in that land, a man righteous in the eyes of all, who had been blessed with great wealth.

2. And his name was Levy, son of Levy, which means one who taketh 15 percent (or we'll work something out).

3. And Levy went unto the courts, which are called tennis, where he met the young ruler of that land, whose name was Ton-y, which is to say "One who getteth away with it, but not for ever".

4. Then said Ton-y unto Levy, "Verily, thou art a rich man and thou knowest many other rich men.

5. "Go unto them privily and say unto them 'The Messiah is here. Give unto him all your money, even unto a millionfold, and your reward shall be great.

6. "'And you will not even have to wait for the Kingdom that is to come.

7. "'For you shall be raised up, and clad in robes of ermine, and you shall be crowned with coronets and you shall sit in the House of the Lords forever.'"

8. And Levy heard this, and did even as his master had commanded.

9. And soon the coffers of the ruler of that land were filled with gifts of shekels, which are called "loans" if anyone asks.

10. But, lo, there was murmuring in the land, and people began to say, one unto another, how has this come to pass that the House of the Lords is filled with common moneylenders and even the vendors of vindaloo?

11. Can it be, they asked, that the ruler of the land hath been granting his favours in exchange for gold and silver?

12. And the ruler heard the cry of the people and was sore afraid. For he feareth the knock on the door in the hours of darkness, when the desert fox stalketh the unwary chicken.

13. And the ruler saith unto the people, "I knoweth nothing of this. For I am a guy that is called straight.

14. "If thou lookest for an guilty man, then thou needest look no further than the House of Levy."

15. And the officers came privily by night to arrest Levy.

16. And Levy waxed wroth, saying, "Knowest thou not who I am? For I am the Lord Levy, friend of Ton-y.

17. "And verily I know where the bodies are buried, if thou catchest my drift."

18. And darkness fell upon the land. And it was now the turn of Ton-y to be sore afraid.

A Statement From Channel Four

IT HAS been brought to our attention that in the quiz show segment 'You Say, We Pay', *The Richard and Judy Show* has been cheating viewers by encouraging them to ring in long after the contest has closed.

In response to this, Channel 4 has set up a phone line in which any viewers affected by the rigged quiz can call in and win themselves £100 by answering the following simple question – Channel 4 is:

A. A squalid and grotesque self parody of the channel it was originally set up to be

B. A banana

C. Cheese

D. Milk

Ring now – it's already too late to win!

Calls charged at £7.50 a minute off peak, £39 a minute all other times.

"Can you find the words hidden in our puzzle?"

OSCAR FOR 'QUEEN'

by Our Showbusiness Staff
Lunchtime O'Drivel

LIZ WINDSOR, 82, last night won an Oscar for her role playing the Queen of England.

"It is an astonishing performance," said the Academy

Award citation. "Everything is totally convincing – the accent, the clothes, the waving. It's as if she had been born to play the part." *(Cont. p. 94)*

(Cont. p. 94)

New-Look House Of Lords

You Decide

Which of the following options do you most favour as the way forward to a modernised second chamber?

1. 100% elected
2. 100% appointed
3. 80% elected, 20% grapefruit segments *(Is this right?)*
4. 40% elected, 60% crooks
5. Celebrity House of Lords – You vote them out (Hosted by Davina McCall)
6. 0-60 in 9 seconds
7. Tottenham 3, Chelsea 3
8. 70% viscose, 20% nylon, 10% cotton
9. Nutritional information 475 calories, 20% gluten
10. Lord Archer, sitting on his own

(That's enough Lords. Ed.)

HURLEY WEDDING Day 94

by Our Liz Hurley Staff
Phil Acres

AND still it goes on. As weary guests assembled for yet another dinner in the fabled fort of Mumbo Jumbai in the desert kingdom of Uttar Bordom, many revellers had lost hope that they would ever return to their loved ones.

Wedding to end all weddings

As the bride changed into her 289th outfit and the groom appeared in a bejewelled carriage drawn by tigers and peacocks, one guest confessed "I can't take any more. It's relentless, 24-hour rose petals, pink champagne and vocal tributes from Elton John." She sobbed, "I always cry at weddings but not usually from boredom."

But their was no respite as the extravaganza moved on to yet another venue with a Black-tie-meets-Bollywood themed party on the moon.

Going over the top

"They said it would all be over by Christmas," said another wedding-hardened veteran, "but at this point in time we still have no exit strategy. To be honest it's Hello on earth." (continued for ever.)

WEDDING OF THE CENTURY

 How They Are Related

Elizabeth The First	Hugh Grant
Elizabeth The Second	Hugh Hee
Helen The Mirren	Hugh Knows
Elizabeth The Taylor	Hugh Cares
Elizabeth The Hurley	**Hugh Snext**

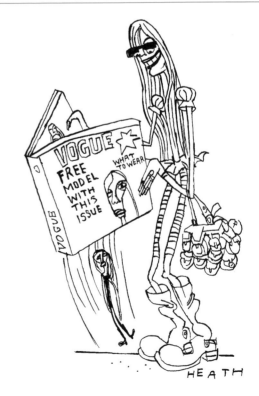

BLAIR: THE HAND OF HIS-CRONY!

...and then they feel your collar like this

ACME BLUE PLAQUES

TONY BLAIR Li ed here 1997–2007

"We've got that ready for Downing Street"

THE ALTERNATIVE VOICE

DAVE LIVINGSPART

(Co-Chair of the Peckham & Camberwell Anti-Trident Pro-Cannabis Ban The Routemaster and Pro-Hugo-Chavez World Alliance).

Once again it is totally sickening to see the white supremacist and Christian bigot William Wilberforce being feted by the media for his so-called abolition of slavery, whereas, as is well known, the entire British Establishment connived in these genocidal atrocities for many centuries until forced to make a massive U-turn by the armed resistance movements led by the slaves themselves, who, having read Marx, Engels etc, rose up as one to throw off the hated yoke of patriarchal mercantile imperialism which no one had done more than Wilberforce to propagate er.. and that is why every white person should not only apologise and offer their houses as reparation to any black persons living in their community but should string themselves up for it is, frankly, to my mind, the only language they understand. I had that Robert Mugabe in the back of the cab the other day, very clever man and totally maligned by the white racist Colonialist media who cannot accept a black man selling his own people into slavery... er...

© A. Taxi Driver 2007.

Eye Grand Apology Offer

What would <u>YOU</u> like us to apologise for?

SIMPLY tick the relevant box and we will issue a heartfelt sincere and unqualified apology on your behalf.

- ☐ The Slave Trade
- ☐ The Crusades
- ☐ The Sinking of the Titanic
- ☐ The Peasants' Revolt
- ☐ Global Warming
- ☐ The Black Death
- ☐ Channel 4
- ☐ Bird Flu
- ☐ Suez
- ☐ England 0 Israel 0
- ☐ The Battle of Agincourt
- ☐ Sir Peregrine Worsthorne

IF YOU would like us to apologise for something you didn't do, just go to our apology website and add your name to the lists of thousands who have already expressed their sorrow and guilt at various events that have taken place throughout history.

ADVERTISEMENT

WHITE NOSE DAY

Celebrities get together to raise money to help the impoverished cocaine producers of the third world. Join them as they support projects in Colombia, Afghanistan, and London's Groucho Club.

★ Starring **Kate Moss**, TV's **Russell Brand** and many more showbiz cokeheads!

In The American Courts

The State of Illinois v. Lord Black of Doublecross before Her Honour Mrs Judge Cockleburger III

Mrs Judge Cockleburger: My fellow Americans, this is gonna be one helluva case! Yes, siree. We got the high life, we got the low life. We even got Mrs Black the Second!

(Enter left The State of Illinois Supreme Court Majorettes, singing "Chicago, Chicago, One helluva town! Lord Black, Lord Black, We're sending you down!".)

(Wild applause from jury.)

Judge Cockleburger: And now introducing the stars of the show! Ladies and gentlemen of the jury, please put your hands together for the Chief Prosecuting Counsel of the great State of Illinois, Mr Al Catraz!

(Applause)

And in the red corner, Counsel for the Defence, Mr Hiram Greenbucks!

(Applause)

And finally, skulking there in the

ANGELINA JOLIE ADOPTS ANOTHER BABY

I've called him Pax Thien, which roughly translates as "up yours Madonna, I saw him first"

dock like a low-down coyote *(© Rev. Dubya Bush)*, you see the English Lord, Mr High-and-Mighty Black.

Greenbucks: Objection, Your Honour. I would like to address the jury.

Mrs Judge Cockleburger: Take it away, Hiram!

Greenbucks: My client is no high-and-mighty British Lordship, as Your Honour suggests. He is just a humble, ornery Canadian lumberjack who likes to be known to his friends as plain "Conman". I'm sorry, I'll read that again. He likes to be known as plain "Conrad".

Foreman of the Jury: We find Lord Conrad guilty as hell.

Cockleburger: All in good time! And it's now time for a word from our sponsor.

(Commercial break for deep-pan pizzas, lager beer and haemorrhoid cream)

Cockleburger: Welcome back to the trial of the century! And it's time to hear the opening speech from our honourable State Prosecuting Attorney Mr Catraz. Take it away, Al.

Al Catraz: Ladies and gentlemen of the jury, the tale you are about to hear will shock you to the roots of your being. It is an epic saga of larceny, greed and avarice, perpetrated by the man you see sitting there before you, the Grand Old Duke of Black, 4,017th in line to the throne of Buckingham Castle in England.

(The Illinois Junior High Freshmen Dancers, dressed as Beefeaters, come on to sing "Money Makes the world go around")

Mr Catraz: You will hear how Lord Blackadder and his scarlet woman, the Countess Barbara of Amiel...

Lady Black *(seated in gallery, demurely dressed as Dorothy from Wizard of Oz and looking not a day over 66)*: Scumbag! Vermin! Bastard!

Cockleburger: Silence in court. I will not have this courtroom turned into a circus.

(Enter troop of elephants holding placards in their trunks, spelling out the message "O.J. Black is innocent")

Catraz: Ladies and gentlemen of the jury, as I was saying, you will hear how these two outlaws, this latter-day version of Bonnie and Clyde, systematically robbed the poor, innocent shareholders of Bollinger International, in order to finance a spending spree not seen since the days of Cleopatra. A madcap crazy whirl of private jets, fancy limousines, champagne and caviar for breakfast, whole cupboards full of designer shoes, fabulous holidays on remote tropical paradise islands, Louis Vuitton suitcases crammed with precious jewels and warehouses full of unsold copies of the Daily Telegraph. Nothing was too extravagant for Milord Aristoblack and his Marie Antoinette, Dame Barbara Cartland. So let me take you through this highly complex trail of deception,

chicanery, double-dealing, embezzlement and fraud.

(Points to huge screen showing picture of Lord Black in striped jumper holding bag marked "Swag")

We are looking at the tangled affairs of no fewer than 487 interlocking companies. At one end we have Bollinger International, with its 79 percent holding in Tollinger International, with its 83 percent holding in Mollinger, Nassau, itself a 92 percent part-owned subsidiary of Kissinger, Cayman Islands, which in turn was controlled by the Toronto Stone and Gravel Co. Inc, in which Lord Black and his wife were the sole shareholders.

Foreman of Jury: Where does a fella get to eat around here?

Mr Greenbucks *(for Lord Black)*: Your Honour, it must be my turn now. So I'd like to call the guy you've all been writing to hear, the big man himself, "Honest Con" of Flat 15, 4672 Saskatchewan Avenue, Moosejaw, Manitoba.

Black: Never before in history has any courtroom been treated to such a pusillanimous, preposterous and pitiful farrago of ignorant poltroonery. Or what the great Talleyrand might have called "the mendacious matter of moral mire".

Foreman of Jury: Can we have an interpreter, please?

Black: This entire case is nothing more than a concoction of calumnies, put together by envious lickspittles and mean-minded midgets, enraged by the genius of a man whose boots they are not worthy to lick and who has bestridden the stage of the world like no one since the great Napoleon Bonaparte, whom I am proud to call my friend!

(Applause. Lake Michigan High School Orchestra strikes up 1812 Overture [arr. Irving Berlin], complete with cannons and Bells of Moscow and fireworks, courtesy of the Bora Bora Pyrotechnic Company [Afghanistan])

Case to be continued...

A DISGRACE TO CRICKET

by **Phil Glass**, Our Man In The Bar With The Tequila Slammer And The Rum Punch Chaser

DRUNK AND USELESS. There's no other way to describe this lamentable performance by someone who should know better. The sight of a grown man drinking himself into a stupor is not a pretty one.

And the inevitable result of this excess is a woeful display of inaccuracy, sloppiness and sheer lack of professionalism in the most important cricket tournament in the world.

Yes, I can only apologise. I'm drunk and this column is uesless. I've let myself down, my team down and my trousers down. Send me home now.

© All newspapers

GLENDA SLAGG

FLEET STREET'S WICKED MAIDEN! (GEDDIT?!)

■ FREDDIE FLINTOFF!!?! What a disgrace!!?? No wonder England keep getting beaten when Four-X Fred is out all night getting hammered – and I don't mean by Bermuda (Geddit!?). Freddie can't even take out a pedalo without falling into the drink!?! Geddit?!? What must kiddies think when they see their hero a-boozin' and a-losin'??!! Howzzat?! You're out! And about time too!?! Flint-Off Andy!? Geddit?!?

■ FREDDIE FLINTOFF!!?! What's all the fuss about?! So he likes a drink! Who doesn't?!? He's only human. What sort of country are we when a young lad can't even have a swift pint or two of rum without the stuffed-shirt brigade coming down on him like a ton of bricks!?! Oi, Mr Killjoy – leave our Fred alone!?! If he wants to fall off a pedalo in the middle of the night, good luck to him!?!

■ DIDYA see the Chancellor's Missus in her mini-skirt and high heels outside No. 11?!? Blimey!!? Who does she think she is – Kate Moss or what?!? Take a tip from Auntie Glenda, sweetheart, stick to the M&S Middleaged Mum range – no offence!?! – and leave the glamour to Cherie Blair!?!

■ HATS OFF to Gordon's Gorgeous Gal?! Sarah Brown I'm talkin' about, stoopid!?! Out go the frowsty frocks and sensible shoes from M&S – in come the sassy microskirt and knock 'em dead shoes!?! Eat your heart out, dumpy Cherie Blair!?! No wonder the guys were a-dribblin' and a-scribblin'?!? All together now – "Knees Out Mother Brown"!?!! Geddit?!!?!

■ HERE THEY ARE – Glenda's Budget-Time Beaux:

● **Edward Heathcote Amery** – the *Mail*'s Munchy Money Maestro!?!
● **Simon Heffer** – the *Telegraph*'s Mr Sex!?!
● **George Pascoe-Watson** – the *Sun*'s Political Editor?!? Don't laugh, Mister, he's for real!?!?

Byeeee!!!

● Read Glenda's blog on www.fleetstreetsfinest.co.uk. Should Freddie be sacked or given a knighthood? Let's hear your views! Or, if you don't have any, text us anyway on 87431. Or do you have any amusing photographs of Ricky Ponting? Or do you have a favourite recipe? Join the debate on www.fillupthepaper.com.

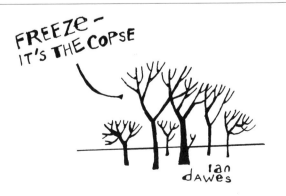

FREEZE – IT'S THE COPSE

ian dawes

SAYS

TIME TO CRACK DOWN ON SICK PEDALOS

THESE vile pedalo scum have now infiltrated the world of sport, hoping to lure young cricketers out to sea for their evil purposes (Is this right? Ed). Now we name and shame those evil pedalos who prey on our lads.

Vile: No 78

Do you know of any dangerous pedalos lurking near you? Call our Rebekah on the Pedalo Hotline 0798534787 and we'll organise a group of vigilantes to burn them!

HELLO! BUYS ROONEY WEDDING FOR £1.5M

Does that include the family brawl afterwards?

POPE MEETS PUTIN

Got any murders to confess?

Perhaps over a plate of sushi, Your Holiness

Mary Ann Bighead

Don't stop me flying around the world being clever!

They say travel broadens the mind – which in my case takes some doing – but it's true! I've flown to more countries than you have and everywhere I've been not only have I learnt something to make me even cleverer but the local people have benefited immeasurably from meeting someone as clever as me.

When I was going round the world writing a column for this newspaper (*What I Did On My Holidays and You Didn't*) I went to Nowheresville, Arizona in America. Everybody thought I was wonderful.

"We love the way you talk. It's different from us," they all said to me. "And the way *you* talk is different from me," I pointed out, "Because I am very clever and you aren't."

This had never occurred to them before which is a perfect example of the long term benefits of allowing the Bighead family to carry on travelling.

And don't worry about carbon emissions because I've cleverly planted a whole forest of trees in Wales in the Valley of Lleverllogs.

© Mary Ann Bighead

49

In The Courts

An inquest into the death of the late Diana, Princess of Hearts, and Mr Dodi Fugger, before Her Honour Dame Butler-Slosselcarrot

Dame Slosselcarrot *(for it is she)*: I think the quickest way to get this ridiculous and wasteful inquest over with is for me to hear it on my own, without all the silly business of calling a jury.

Mr Michael Hugefee QC *(for Mr Al Fugger)*: Objection, Your Honour. My client, Mr Al Fugger, a highly-respected Egyptian conman, cannot accept Your Ladyship's proposal. He believes that a single judge, however elderly and decrepit she may be, is unlikely to be persuaded by his farrago of lies. Yet a jury of twelve good persons and true is much more likely to be taken in by his nonsensical and mendacious version of events, particularly if they are readers of the Daily Express.

Dame Slosselcarrot: Are you suggesting, Mr Hugefee, that I am in the pay of the Duke of Edinburgh? *(Laughter)*

Hugefee: Indeed I am, Your Honour. Ipsissima verba, as we lawyers like to say! Can I refer you to Mr Fugger's sworn affidavit in Bundle B in which he says, "I will fuggin' prove that this fuggin' old bat is working for fuggin' MI6 and was the fuggin' driver of the white Fiat Uno".

This will be our case, I respectfully submit, and I shall be calling a number of witnesses to verify these facts.

Dame Slosselcarrot: These are indeed powerful arguments, Mr Hugefee, or so the Judges at the High Court seem to think. I am therefore minded to summon a jury, as you so eloquently suggest; so that all the world may see that even the most stupid of jurors is unlikely to be swayed by such a tissue of paranoid fabrications.

Hugefee: I am indebted to you, Your Ladyship, and indeed to Mr Fugger, for giving me such a huge sum of money to talk this nonsense!

Slosselcarrot: I have examined 159 different reports into the unfortunate events of 10 years ago, and I am bound to say that there is not a jot or scintilla of evidence to support your client's allegations – namely that the Duke of Edinburgh, aided and abetted by MI6, Smersh, Spectre and Mr Darth Vader, materialised from a spaceship inside the fatal tunnel of Pont D'Alma in order to effect the murder of the secretly married Diana, Princess of Wales, who was already pregnant with the first Muslim King of England: the Pharaoh Fayed Windsor the First.

Hugefee: I assure Your Ladyship that we have a wealth of new evidence to support every one of these claims. Indeed we have so much evidence that it will take six months just to find it on the internet!

This is why my client requests an adjournment, so that the whole matter can roll on for another six months and I can therefore collect a number of very welcome 'refreshers'.

Dame Slosselcarrot: Again, I am persuaded by the sagacity of your arguments, Mr Hugefee, and furthermore that will give me an opportunity to take a brief retirement cruise round the world – including, may I say, Mr Fugger, a visit to your native pyramids!

Fugger: If you're going to Cairo, lady, you go see my cousin. He sell carpets, very nice, very cheap. You tell him Fuggin' Fugger sent you, and he give you very good price!!

Slosselcarrot: I am indebted to you, Mr Fayed. This court is now adjourned for six months.

New passport guidelines: help with photographs

| Too close | Not far away enough | Too frightening | Too old |
| Busy background | Another person in picture | Avoiding camera | Totally unacceptable |

'I STILL LOVE PAUL'S MONEY'
says Heather

by our Showbiz Staff **Lies R. Minnelli**

THE estranged wife of former Beatle Sir Paul McCartney last night blamed the lawyers for her separation from his bank account.

Talking on American television's "Good Morning Wyo-ming" she told anchorman Larry Humbug, "The money and I still have a great relationship. I never wanted to lose the money. It's only the lawyers who are trying to get between me and Macca's loot."

Full story and pictures **p. 94**

An Apology by Private Eye

IN RECENT years, Private Eye may have suggested that "Taking the Independent" was a harmless leisure activity on a par with smoking or drinking and that even when taken every day was unlikely to cause longterm ill effects.

Cannabis independica

However, we now realise that the new strain of Independent (known as "Junk") is much stronger and, if indulged in too frequently, can lead to depression, psychosis and serious rotting of the brain.

We would like to apologise for this very serious misjudgement on our part and now support legislation which would reclassify the Independent as a Class Z newspaper, the consumption and distribution of which should be prohibited.

ROSIE BOREPOT writes ■ Why I still believe in the freedom to smoke the Independent whatever the experts say... **94**

Those British Press Awards

(continued from page one)

press gazette

Best Free Wallchart

● **The Grauniad**
British Barrel Bottoms (No 94)

Best Free DVD

● **The Daily Telegraph**
"They Flew to Bruges" Disappointing 1973 remake of wartime classic starring Oliver Reed in the Kenneth More role of Squadron Leader "Chalkie" Chalkington. Directed by Michael Winner.

Best Free CD

● **Daily Mail**
"Sprechen Zie Walloon!" Interactive Listen 'n' Learn course. Fluent Flemish in just 6 weeks!

Best Shower Unit Insert

● **The Sunday Times**
Aquafresh Shower Solutions, Runcorn. Glossy A4 "Edvertisement Feature" on the new Power Nozzle 3000 range.

Best Eurostar Offer

● **The Observer**
2 for 1 voucher deal choice of Lille or Brussels departing Ashford with booze stop at Calais' celebrated "Monde de Booze" Hypermarche Experience.

Sudoku of the Year

● **Daily Express**
Kamikaze No. 73248. Level: Easy.

(That's enough recognition for top quality journalism in the National Press. Ed)

SOLDIER HONOURED

by Our Military Correspondent **Victoria Cross**

LIEUTENANT Harry Windsor of the Booze & Royals Regiment is to receive one of the highest military honours, The Order of the Seven Vodkas, following an engagement in the early hours at the notoriously dangerous enemy encampment at Boujis.

Says the citation: "The unarmed Lieutenant Windsor singlehandedly attacked an enemy snapper who was carrying a fully loaded Nikon automatic. Lt Windsor pursued the enemy beyond the call of nature whilst the snapper took several shots at him.

Windsor bravely ran forward shouting obscenities and grappled with his assailant, giving his all before collapsing fatally drunk into the gutter. He was later dragged to safety by members of the elite royal minder squad."

The citation concludes, "Seldom has a young officer showed such exemplary stupidity. We recommend he be court martialled *(surely shome mistake)*.

WOMAN DOESN'T HAVE FLING WITH CHRIS TARRANT

by Our Media Staff **Milly Onair**

A 45-year-old woman yesterday sensationally claimed that she and Chris Tarrant were not having an affair.

The woman told reporters, "Yes, it's true. TV millionaire Chris Tarrant and I have not slept together and are not even just good friends. He didn't meet me in a wine bar and then didn't install me in a love nest near his home".

The woman's claims were, however, dismissed by Mr Tarrant as "pure fantasy".

But his troubles were made worse when another 45-year-old woman claimed that it was actually she who was not sleeping with the multi-billionaire lothario.

"I thought I was the only woman not in Chris Tarrant's life," she said. "The discovery that there is someone else not sharing intimate trysts with the TV multi-trillionaire has come as a terrible shock."

The last word, however, went to Ingrid Tarrant, the multi-zillionaire presenter's ex-wife.

"There is only one woman not sleeping with that bastard and it's me."

"Gentlemen, shall we join the bitches?"

POLICE LOG

Neasden Central Police Station

0815 hrs Disciplinary proceedings begin in the case of PC Perivale, who is charged with wilfully going on patrol whilst neglecting to complete his paperwork duties. The PC had on 21 March been observed leaving the police station during office hours and proceeding down the street towards the Bluetooth Shopping Mall. When he was stopped by a passing patrol car containing PCs Chalfont and Latimer and asked "What the hell are you doing?", PC Perivale replied, "I am on the beat keeping an eye open for anything suspicious."

PC Perivale was then informed that this was a gross breach of station discipline which could lead to his suspension, unless he was able to prove discrimination on grounds of ethnicity or religion.

Details of the charge against PC Perivale were duly logged on forms AB/4231, PSQ/61, FSB/2007 and PM/29, and submitted to the Disciplinary Management Unit for processing prior to onward referral to the Management Disciplinary Unit.

1300 hrs Full station alert on receipt of a 999 message from a member of staff at the Shirley Williams Primary School in Poundstretcher Lane. It had been reported that a serious hate-crime had been perpetrated by one pupil of the school against another. An armed response unit was despatched to the school, where it was discovered that Child X had sent Child Y a text message reading "Kev u r a gayboy'. Child X was taken into custody after a brief struggle and subjected to interrogation at the station under the Police and Criminal Evidence Act.

As a result of information extracted from Child X, a second armed response unit was sent to his home address at 412B Spudulike Grove, where his parents were arrested and charged with conspiring to condone a homophobic hate-crime.

When the father of Child X verbally resisted arrest with the offensive remark "I have no idea what you are talking about", he was pacified with a 50,000-volt taser device, which coincided with his premature demise from unrelated causes.

Fortunately the officers involved, PCs Bethnal and Green, were able to claim a month's overtime for the completion of the 24,612 forms that were required in connection with the incident referred to above.

1634 hrs While the station staff were engaged in high-priority police duties, a number of calls had been received on the station answerphones reporting various incidents in the Neasden area, including 14 stabbings, 12 drive-by shootings and a number of alleged acts of rape. Regrettably the messages had to be deleted owing to cutbacks on answerphone tape required under the station's latest budgetary control, rendering further police action unnecessary.

Nursery Times

Friday, March 30, 2007

HAMELIN COUNCIL DEFENDS FORTNIGHTLY RUBBISH COLLECTION

by Our Environmental Staff **Billie Pied-Piper**

THE local council of Hamelin are sticking by their controversial decision to stop weekly rubbish collections. The council claim that the new fortnightly service will force residents to compost and recycle waste, thus making the operation more environmentally friendly.

Residents, however, have expressed fears that the cutbacks will lead to the whole town being overrun by rats.

Said the Mayor, "This is ludicrous scaremongering. The one thing that isn't going to happen is a plague of rats running through the streets, scaring dogs and biting children."

He continued, "Any suggestion that the council will end up having to bring in a hugely expensive pest control solution consultant is far-fetched. As is the idea that we would then refuse to pay him, leading to the kidnap of all our children. Trust me. That's not going to happen."

On other pages

"I didn't steal 60 million tarts," says Black of Hearts **2**

Jiminy "One-Day" Cricket found drunk – "My conscience guides me to apologise," he admits **3**

GM fly swallows old woman **94**

IDEA   ECO-IDEA!

TORIES ATTACK LABOUR OVER REFUSE COLLECTION

I've got Rubbish Policies

54

ETHICAL FASHION

How Green Is Your Dressing Gown?

ONCE again Prince Charles leads the way in showing how we can all make a contribution to saving the planet by the way we dress.

Charles's all-purpose "Green Robe" was yesterday unveiled to the press at a special launch in the grounds of Highgrove.

"This robe," the Prince explained, "is incredibly energy-efficient and can be worn 7/24 at any time of day or night.

"By combining the functions of a dressing gown and an overcoat, it saves over 0.05 tonnes of CO_2 emissions every year.

"In addition, by being made of sustainable wool hand-woven from Afghan goats, it saves 200 acres of rainforest which would otherwise be turned into an environmentally damaging tweed suit of the type worn by my father. What a bastard!"

The Prince is expected to join Twiggy in helping M&S to launch a full range of his new carbon-friendly "overgowns" later this year, retailing at £5,400 each.

Insulating thermal scarf to stop heat wastefully escaping

Carbon-neutral buttons made from organically farmed rhinoceros horn

Wellington boots hand-crafted in China from sustainable rubber to minimise carbon footprint

Fully 'composting' pockets in which all waste materials can be turned into plant nutrients

Ancient Hindu holistic symbols representing the balance of man and nature

---

My eBay

luckyheather (32,000,000)

Items I'm Bidding On (1-4 of 4 items)

	Current Price	Postage Cost	Bids
☐ 'How To Win Friends And Influence People' paperback unread			
	£1.99	£1.50	1
☐ Cheap! Designer bag – fake crocodile, tears on outside, fine inside			
	£8.99	£2.99	1
☐ Useful Kitchen Gadget – stops butter melting – works every time!			
	£12.99	£3.00	1
☐ Biography of Yoko Ono, reasonable copy			
	£3.99	£1.50	1

Items I'm Selling (1-4 of 4 items)

	Current Price	Postage Cost	Bids
☐ 'Rumours' make-up set, by Stella McCartney – achieve that natural 'bare-faced' look – includes various lip glosses, but no foundation			
	£25.00	£2.50	0
☐ Authentic tiger-skin rug, genuine reason for sale			
	£5.00	£15.00	0
☐ 'When I'm Sixty-Four' – old Beatle release, single, slightly warped			
	£0.50	£2.00	0
☐ 'Gold Diggers of 1933' DVD – bought in error			
	£1.00	£1.00	0

RALPH FIENNES FLIES UNDONE
(surely 'Qantas'? Ed)

I'm in Monkey Business Class

Could you please unfasten your belt, sir?

THEN

BANG! BANG! YOU'RE DEAD!

YOU GOT ME!

NOW

RESPECT!

ENGLAND TEAM KNOCKED OUT BY NO-HOPERS IRAN

by Our Cricketing Staff **W.G. Disgrace**

The England Squad in their smart-casual new kit designed by Giorgio Ahmanidinejacket

THE ENGLAND sailing team flew home today after a shock defeat at the hands of the 100-1 outsiders Iran.

Said a disappointed skipper Captain Cornwall, "We had the firepower and the talent, but on the day we failed to focus. We are gutted obviously but to give the Iranians credit they did play a blinder, especially Ahmadinejad."

Barmy Ahmadinejad

He continued, "The media had written him off as a clown but there was nothing funny about the way he tied our team up and bamboozled us with his superior spin."

As the team flew back into Heathrow to be greeted by the Prime Minister there were some tough questions to answer about their performance.

Caught Behind

Why did they give in so easily? Had they been properly prepared? Were they too over confident?

These are the urgent issues which must be addressed as we prepare for the next World War.

Late score: England 15 all out (Iran stopped play)

THE DEATH OF NELSON – MODERN NAVY STYLE

Late Iran News

GEORGE BUSH has launched a savage attack on Iran after it captured fifteen British sailors and marines.

"The Iranians really should have put their prisoners in manacles and orange jumpsuits and started torturing them," insisted the President.

"Instead, they let them go. This shows a complete disregard for the Geneva Convention as re-written by me."

"Try it again, General – 'This urgent surge will purge the insurgent scourge'"

'I NEVER MET WILSON' Marcia's Shock Claim

by Our BBC Staff **Michael White-Flag**

LADY FALKENDER, formerly Marcia Williams, claimed today that she had never met the Prime Minister who she served as private and political secretary for 30 years.

Speaking yesterday from the Lavender Old People's Home in Kagan Lane she said, "The BBC have been trying to portray me as someone who worked for Harold Wilson.

"This is an appalling slur and it is a great relief to me that the BBC have given me a huge cheque to see me through my declining years."

No Wheen, No Fee

This was a reference to the rumoured £7 million that the BBC has agreed to pay Lady Falkender for mentioning her name in various news bulletins over the last 40 years.

Said a spokesman for the BBC, "We are glad to have had this opportunity to put the record straight and we are delighted to hand over this enormous cheque to Lady Falkender's lawyers, Messrs Carter-Fuck and Partners for no good reason at all."

Late News

The late Mr Carter-Fuck is to receive a posthumous peerage from the late Lord Wilson of Gannex for services to censorship.

Join the Debate

Which of these jokes would you most like to see in a bubble on the above picture?

a) Wilson: Any chance of a Falkender?

b) Marcia: Is that a pound in your pocket or are you just pleased to see me?

c) Wilson: (smoking pipe not shown in picture) I like a bit of old shag.

Email us now on **wislonfalkbender@ naughtygnome.co.uk**

That Carter-Fuck Bill in Full

For writing threatening letter to BBC	**£300,000**
For putting letter in envelope	**£200,000**
For stamp	**32p**
For senior partner's time in licking stamp @ £40,000 per hour x 3	**£120,000**
For accepting huge cheque from BBC lawyers Messrs Cowardy, Cowardy and Custard	**£500,000**
For adding up the above sums	**£1,000,000**
	plus VAT @ 17.5%
Total	**Shall we say £10 million?**

GREAT SPEECHES OF THE 20TH CENTURY

**No 1.
Earl Spencer's historic address to his second wife (2006)**

I'm sorry, darling, I know you've just had a baby and all that but I've been seeing someone else and I want a divorce.

We Spencers have a long and distinguished tradition of behaving like shits and I'm no different It's in the blood. Ask my first wife. She had loads of children before I dumped her! Anyway, I've got to go and have lunch now with my old friend Guppy, his wife's jolly tasty. Aren't the Windsors awful??

© *Earl Spencer 2006.*

Tomorrow: Guardian Editor Alan Rusbridger's historic address to the staff, *"I'm sorry you can't have any more money because I've got it all."*

PUSHY PARENTS' EVENING

"She's doing extremely well, thank you. She's a very bright girl... a genius, actually"

DIARY
MELVYN BRAGG MEETS GEORGE MICHAEL

MELVYN: Michael George shot to fame as a leading member of the trio Whim! As a signwriter, sorry, songwriter, he has achieved international success by writing acclaimed songs such as um er, by writing several um famous songs. Michael George is now internationally acknowledged as a erm, as a leading erm, singer, indeed as one of the most singery and singerest singers, erm, of his generation. On the eve of his first World Tour since his last, Michael George gave us this exclusive insight into the way he erm...

* * *

GEORGE: Super to see you, Melvyn! How you doin'? Ooh, you smell nice! Mmmm...doesn't he smell nice, boys?

MELVYN: Can we start with the early days, Michael. You began life, am I right in thinking, in the womb?

GEORGE: Too right, Melvyn. Frankly I've never been so frustrated, all cooped up in there, with such terrible lighting, and so uncomfabaw, without any real means of expressing myself as a gay foetus, I mean I was forced to just lie there for months on end looking like goodness knows what, it was so humiliating and I can't bear to be negative about anything in this world but I had this great sense of darkness in there and I didn't really know how I was going to emerge and that's kind of upsetting for a major creative artist like myself, and then when I did come out, thank you very much, I was just made to lie there in a pair of nappies without any form of public redress because at that stage I wasn't able or allowed to speak out, it was so unfair, and you know as a gay baby wanting to lead a gay baby's lifestyle according to my own principles without compromising my identity I was overwhelmed by this terrible sense of the injustice of it all, it was just horrific.

MELVYN: *Zzzzzzz. Zzzzzzzz. (wakes with a start)* Where am I? Who are you? Where were

we?! Yes! Can we start with the early days, Michael. You began life, am I right in thinking, as a – no sorry. Let's move on. After being a foetus and then a baby for – what? one or two years – you then, am I right in thinking, proceeded to become a child, in your case a boy?

GEORGE: Yes, Melvyn, I was indeed a child in those early years, forced by this society we live in to go around dressed as a child and behaving as a child and it was an experience that I wouldn't wish on anyone, it was cruel, you see I was so vownrabaw, it was really eating me up, when all I wanted was my dignity and my self-determination and the whole process of like being a child made me understand something about how this government really manipulates us into believing – sorry Melvyn, can we stop for a sec? You know what? I'm feeling a bit sweaty. Do I look sweaty to you, Melvyn? Now, be honest!

MELVYN: Hm?

GEORGE: D'you know, Melvyn, I'm feeling a bit sweaty?

MELVYN: Um. No. Remind me. How does it go?

* * *

MELVYN: Your song, "Hey, Hump Me, Hump Me, Baby, I'm Your Kinda Guy" was written as a response to the invasion of Iraq.

GEORGE: I was that livid, I really was, Melvyn. It was when I heard that Tony was going to invaderate Iraq. Honestly, that guy had no business to, I don't care if he is Prime Minister or whatever! As a sexually active gay man, I felt that no-one should put up with this kind of invasion, I mean, how would YOU feel if one morning there was a ding-dong on your doorbell and all sorts of soldiers and what-not just sort of marched their way in uninvited and without their VIP passes or anything? I mean, it all comes back to human nature, doesn't it, Melvyn? So I thought, I'm not having this, this calls for a protest, and so I thought I'd show my anger against the whole war thing in a very very smooth, very very protesty, very very sexy sort of song, and I'd like to sing it for you all now.

MELVYN: *Zzzzzz.* Sorry?

GEORGE: I'd love to sing it for you all now.

MELVYN: Sing what?

GEORGE: My protesty song, silly!

MELVYN: That would be tremendous. So would it be true to say that what are you saying is that it would be true to say that you are a um singer as well as a signwriter?

GEORGE: Yes, silly!

MELVYN: That's extraordinary. You certainly kept that quiet!

GEORGE *(singing):* "Oooooh! Hey, hump me, hump me, hump me, baby! I'm your kinda guy! And if you go and invade Iraq again You'll only make me cry! Ooooh! Hump me! Ooooh! Ooooh!"

* * *

GEORGE: And the result of my protest? Rumsfeld gets the push! The Americans now know that the next time they lift a finger against a foreign country, they'll have George Michael and his fanbase to deal with. In their eyes, I am now officially part of the problem. It's not something they'll ever forgive. That's why the second I'm found cruising on Hampstead Heath as part of a sexually active gay male lifestyle, the White House is straight on the phone to Murdoch ordering him to print the news throughout the world. Friends told me I was mad to take on the American war machine, but that's the kind of guy I am – if I want to cruise in a dignified manner as part of a gay male lifestyle, then I'm not going to let Dick Cheney stop me by threatening to invade Hampstead Heath and bomb me sky-high, thank you very much, Melvyn. I'm now 43 years old, would you believe, and no matter what happens – actually, sorry, Melvyn, can we stop a mo? I'm getting really ever so sweaty! Melvyn? Melvyn?

MELVYN: *Zzzzz.* Eh? Eh? Where am I? This morning on In Your Time, we investigate the nature and role of Manichaean Dualism in 3rd century Persia.

GEORGE: "Squeeze me, squeeze me, you sexy thing! I don't wannna cause no disruption, So – oooh! – let me be your weapon of mass destruction! Oooh! Oooh! Oooh!"

As told to CRAIG BROWN

WHY DID KATE AND WILLS SPLIT?

We don't know.

GLENDA SLAGG

FLEET STREET'S LADY MUCK!?! (GEDDIT?)

■ PRINCE WILLS!!?! What a slimy love rat!!?? How dare he dump the lovely Miss Middleton (aka The People's Kate) as if she was some worn-out dishcloth?! You should be ashamed of yourself, sir, a-gigglin' and a-sniggerin' with your pissed posh pals behind her back – just because her mum says 'toilet' instead of 'lavatory'!?!! WHO BLOODY CARES!!?! Take a tip from Auntie Glenda, Your Royal Snobbiness, and flush yourself down the toilet!!?!

■ HATS OFF to Prince William!!?! He's had the courage to do the decent thing and not keep his girlfriend Kate hanging around waiting for him to pop the question!?!! What young man in modern Britain gets hitched at 24, for Gawd's sake?!? NO ONE!!!?! Like any other red-blooded young buck, Wills needs to sow his wild oats before he walks down the aisle with Miss Right. Good for you, sire, and happy hunting in Boujis!?!!?

■ THE NATION's hearts go out to lovely Kate Middleton, the demure English rose who never lost her dignity amidst the Royal razzamatazz!!?! Now she's been chucked out like an old dishcloth, and sits a-sighin' and a-sobbin' as she dreams of what might have been!?! Boo-hoo-hoo!?! Forgive me fellas if I have a lil weep into my hankie!?! But take a tip from auntie Glenda, Kate – you're better off without him?!?? One Middleton is worth a hundred Windsors any day – and that's official!!?!

■ QUEEN KATE Middleton!?!! Don't make me laugh!?!! Who did she think she was kidding, measuring up the throne of England when she was a common shop girl on the make!?!! And you know what? Her mother can't even spell the word 'toilet'!!?!! WHAT'S THE WORLD COMING TO, FOR GAWD'S SAKE!!?!

■ HERE THEY ARE – Glenda's Maypole Machos:

● **Dave Miliband.** He's the 'coming man'!?! Geddit!?!

● **Ed Balls** – say no more!!?!

● **Michael Vaughan.** Can't score, love?! I'll sort you out!!?!

Byeeee!!!

"You only have to acknowledge your inner child. You don't have to dress up in his clothes"

Lines On The Separation Of His Royal Highness Prince William And Miss Kate Middleton

by the late Poet Laureate **Sir John Betjeman**

How To Get On In Society

A Royal Wedding, so why should we spoil it
Just because Kate's mum chews gum and says 'toilet'?
I think Kate would have made a right Royal wife
Even if Carole says 'Pardon' and eats with a fishknife.

(It's not very good is it? Put it in if you like. Cheerio, old bean. J.B.)

WILLS AND KATE SEPARATE

Why I Didn't Have A Clue That This Would Happen

● *The inside story of how I knew nothing about it by Our Royal Reporter PHIL SPACE*

YES, when I said last week that the engagement of Prince William and Kate Middleton was only "days away", it was obvious that nobody tells me anything and that *(You're fired. Ed.)*

How They Are Not Related Any More

William the Conqueror (1066)
|
William the Deedes (1087)
|
Wilhelm the Kaiser (1914-1918)
|
William the Just (1950, as narrated by Martin Jarvis)
|
World Cup William (1966)
|
William the Hague (£800,000 a year)
|
William the Bastard (2007)

Katherine the Great
|
Katherine the Kate
|
Kate the Moss
|
Kathy Come Home
|
Kath 'n' Kim
|
Kiss Me Kate
|
Kate Middleclass

"Oh, come on – do we really need a residents' association?"

WHO ARE THEY, The Upper Class Girls Whom Prince William Is Now Free To Marry?

❶ Lady Poshella Nobbington-Nobbe, youngest daughter of Lord Lordly, the 37th Earl of Urle. Helps run her brother's Mayfair nightclub "Chavs".

❷ The Hon Tatiana Lavatory-Napkin, eldest daughter of ancient land-owning family whose ancestor Guy de Lavatoire-Serviette came over with William the Conqueror

❸ Fruitella Fruitington-Fruitsworth, known as "Fruity" in Royal Circles. Hugely rich, great fun and unencumbered by any GCSEs.

❹ Princess Mercedes Benz von Ribena-Saxon-Drugzen-Rokken-Röll. 14th in line to the throne of the Bavarian principality of Snobenia.

❺ Debretta "Debbo" Featherstone-Hough *(pronounced "Trouserpress")* is the middle daughter of *(That's enough. Ed.)*

Do you think this joke is in bad taste? Do you want to cancel your subscription? Let us know what you think so we don't have to fill the paper ourselves. Simply email us at jointhedebate@dailytelegnome.co.uk

GLENDA SLAGG

■ HATS OFF to Tina Brown!!?! Bubbly bosomy Tina's in town!?! Yes, the Glamorous Gal from the Big Apple is here to promote her sensational page-turner on Princess Di! OK, there are 878 Diana books already which all tell you the same thing!?! Who cares!?! Tina's is the only one that's having a big VIP celebrity party this week!?! See ya there Mister!?! And put the champagne on ice!!?!

■ TINA BROWN – aren'tchasickofher?!?? Blimey!? We thought we'd seen the last of this graspin' go-getter when she crossed the pond with her clapped-out hubby – no offence Sir Harold!?! But, Gawd 'elp us, here she is again a-huffin' and a-puffin' her two-bit tome on the People's Princess!?! Yawn! Yawn! We've read it all before, love, and it wasn't interesting then!?! Take Auntie Glenda's advice, Tina – scarper back to the Big Apple and leave us to drink your champagne in peace!?! Get lost and we'll carry on a-slurpin' and a-burpin' at your expense!?!!

■ THREE CHEERS for the Wags!?! That's 'Wives And Galfriends' to you, Mister!?! Yes, they've all finally tied the knot – so now it's Mr and Mrs Stevie G, Mr and Mrs Terry J, Mr and Mrs One-Of-The-Neville Brothers, and Mr and Mrs The Other Footballer Whose Name We Can't Remember!?! All together now – "Here comes Wayne Rooney in a helicopter!"!?!

■ WAGS!??! SLAGS, I call them!?! That's 'Stupid Lazy and Grasping Slappers' – Geddit?!? No wonder we lost the World Cup when all their hubbies-to-be could think about was how they were going to foot the bill for the million-pound-a-minute receptions!?!! And to cap it all poor Wayne Rooney, the spud-faced nipper, had to fly round the country in a helicopter just to congratulate the blushing brides!?! All together now – "Here Comes The Bill!" Blimey!?!

■ HERE HE IS – Glenda's Midsummer Man of the Month!

● Sir Stephen Richards. He's the Flashing Judge – or rather he isn't?!?? Pity – I wouldn't mind His Ludship giving me a quick peek at his privates on the 8.17 to Waterloo!?!! All rise, Your Honour!?! Geddit!?!!

Byeeeee!!!

"Was the zombies' burial ground mentioned in the Home Information Pack?"

Rossell.

THAT HILARIOUS COMIC RELIEF SKETCH

You're leaving your party and your country in a terrible mess

Am I bovvered? Does my face look bovvered? I'm not bovvered...

Advertisement

MR. BAKED BEAN

JOIN the hilarious antics of Britain's top movie funnyman Hugh Grant in a new slapstick comedy.

Trouble starts when Mr Baked Bean goes out jogging and is then snapped by a photographer!

In no time, Mr Baked Bean has got himself up to his neck in trouble and is on an assault charge! And got himself a whole load more unwanted publicity! You'll laugh! You'll cry! You'll wonder if he's gone mad!

CAST IN FULL

Mr Baked Bean	Colin Firth
Hugh Grant	Rowan Atkinson
Liz Hurley	Jemima Khan
Heinz Baked Beans	Tesco's Own Brand Value Bean-Style Beans

OUTRAGE AT RUBBISH REMOVAL FREQUENCY

by Our Refuse Staff **Osama Wheelie bin Laden**

AS RESIDENTS of Britain went to the polls yesterday there were increasingly angry protests around the country at the schedule of local rubbish removal.

Said one furious householder, "Why are we only allowed to get rid of the rubbish once every four years? It's a disgrace."

Said another, "No wonder the country's in such a mess. We should have dumped all this trash ages ago. Why is it still here?"

Ordure! Ordure!

Pressure groups complain that unwanted garbage has been piling up in local council chambers rotting slowly and then starting to fester. As a result, they claim, rats have been running amok in local government leaving 'a huge stink everywhere'.

Green Has-Bins

However there was no sign that more regular rubbish removal was on the way. Said a Local Government spokesman, "People have got to learn to recycle. Don't just throw us out because we're rubbish, use us again! That way we can save our jobs if not the planet."

"You can only bring out your dead every two weeks now"

NEW OLD SONGS

Oh, my old man's a dustman.
He wears a dustman's cap.
He comes round once a fortnight,
Frankly the service's crap...

EYE HIGHLIGHTS

FILMS

Pirates of the Caribbean 94

YES, they're back! Those thieving pirates from Disney who are going to take your money and sail off leaving you half-dead with boredom, marooned in a creaky old vessel that takes over three hours to get nowhere.

Eye verdict *They should all walk the plank (played by Keira Knightley)*

CHELSEA FLOWER SHOW
Prizewinning design: Traditional English Garden

CRAZY SCENES AS DEMENTED FANS FIGHT OVER KATE MOSS ITEMS

by Our High Street Staff **Philip Greed**

FASHION frenzy erupted yesterday as hundreds of middle-aged men stampeded through central London trying to get Kate Moss items for their newspapers.

Said one screaming editor, Paul Dacre, "I saw the *Evening Standard* had a little Kate Moss number so I had to have one as well." Said another, Robert Thompson, 49, "I don't care what I get, so long as it's got Kate's name in it!" A third, Alan Rubbisher, 51, was the most excited of all, "I don't care if its pants, I just want it!" he said.

Watching teenagers were, however, baffled by this 'Moss Hysteria'. Said one 16-year-old schoolgirl, "Why aren't they in their offices doing their jobs? They shouldn't be allowed in the streets competing to waste their money on

so-called exclusive items from the Kate Moss Collection."

Moss Dross

Nevertheless, the lucky editors were thrilled with their purchases. Said *Telegraph* editor Will Lewis, 37, "This Kate Moss stuff makes us look young, trendy and happening."

Kate Moss's New Line

Der Telegraf Spee
DREI PFENNIGS

FÜHRER'S 'CONCERN' OVER LEGACY

by Our Man In The Bunker
**Professor Hugh Very-Ropey
(later Lord Paul Dacre)**

OUR BELOVED Führer has been telling his inner circle of his "deep concern" that his historic legacy may be overlooked by future generations.

I understand that he has confided in senior Party figures his fear that his many great achievements in rebuilding the country after the dark days of the Thatcher Republic will be overshadowed by the unpopularity of the war, for which many hold him reponsible.

Blair Hitler

"All people go on about is that wretched war," the Führer has reportedly told aides. "No one ever mentions how much I did to improve schools and hospitals – not to mention my historic constitutional reforms, such as

burning down the Reichstag."

The Führer is convinced that in a thousand years' time people will come to see him as the greatest leader his country ever had, even if no one realised it at the time.

"No one," he insists, "will even mention the war. They will merely associate me with public services which are the envy of the world, and with winning the Olympics for Berlin in 1936."

"Why is there nothing about you on MySpace, YouTube or Google? It's like I don't really know you at all!"

NEW-LOOK ULSTER

Fancy a kneecap... I mean 'nightcap'?

SHOULD HARRY GO TO BOUJIS?

by Our Military Staff **Major Hangover**

TOP ARMY BRASS are increasingly worried about the deployment of His Royal Highness Prince Harry in the high-risk zone at Boujis.

"Conditions in the nightclub are pretty hairy," said one fellow officer. "There's a lot of incoming vodka and Harry is a natural target for blonde bombshells."

He continued, "It's not really fair on all the other chaps if Harry is in there because we can't really protect him if we've trying to do our job properly – i.e. get really hammered ourselves."

A veteran of Boujis, Guy Pelly-Silly, 22, disagreed. "Harry is well prepared for night-ops in Kensington," he said. "He's done the training and experienced hundreds of live rounds of champagne and absinthe slammers. It would be a real waste if he was not allowed to see service at Boujis – which is very good actually if you bung Otto a tenner behind the bar!"

On Other Pages

● **Should Princess Beatrice be sent to Boujis instead? Or shouldn't women be on the drinking front line?**

Join the debate at fillournewspaper.co.uk or alternatively don't bother and just get "wankered" instead at boujis.co.uk

Fairy Tales Of Our Time

No. 94

THE BIG BAD WOLFOWITZ

THERE WAS once a Big Bad Wolfowitz whose only interest in life was to go around the world looking for things to blow up.

One day he came across some poor little Iraqis, huddled in their homes made of straw.

He said to them, "Surrender at once, or I'll huff and I'll puff and I'll blow your country up."

And he did!

Fresh from this great triumph, the Big Bad Wolfowitz was promoted to be put in charge of the World Bonk *(surely 'Bank'? Ed)*.

Now his job was to go around the world giving lots of money to poor people to enable them to build more houses of straw.

"This is no fun," said the Big Bad Wolfowitz. "Can't I give the money to my girlfriend instead?"

So he did. And he said to her, "I'll huff and I'll puff and I'll blow your skirt up."

And he did that too.

But eventually everyone noticed what he was up to.

So they all huffed and puffed and thought they should blow him away.

And they did.

So that was the end of the Big Bad Wolfowitz.

Downfall of a Titan

By our City Staff Lunchtime O'Pec

One of the great figures of British industry has been brought low in scenes reminiscent of a Greek tragedy.

They called him a colossus, a prince of capitalists, one of the most brilliant businessmen the world has ever known.

Lord Browne of Madabouttheboy

The secret of his genius lay in his almost uncanny ability to sell large quantities of petrol at a very high price.

This unique skill won him the respect and admiration of the entire civilised world.

Said one awe-struck insider, "John's strategy was worthy of Einstein. He had worked out that there were a lot of people in the world who needed petrol. And he could sell it to them for a large profit."

And yet this mighty Napoleon of the forecourt, this Potentate of Petroleum, perhaps the finest mind ever to spend 40 years sitting behind a desk in BP, has been brought low by a drama worthy of the pen of Sophocles himself.

Who could have foreseen that this Sultan of the Service Stations, this Goliath of Gasoline, this Rajah of Rent Boys *(surely some mistake? Ed.)* (cont. p. 94)

BROWNE AND CHEVALIER: SHAMEFUL SECRET

Are you a friend of Dorothy?

No, I'm a friend of Tony

♪ Zank 'eaven for leetle boys

BROWN REPUTATION IN TATTERS

by Our Scotland Correspondent **Maurice Chevalier**

GORDON Brown's reputation with voters was in tatters last night after he was forced to admit that he had lied in the papers about his long-term relationship with a glamorous younger man, Tony Blair.

"I now admit that when I described Tony in that interview in the *Sun* as a "great Prime Minister" I was lying through my teeth" an ashamed Gordon Brown told reporters on Friday. "Tony had blackmailed me into lying by threatening to hang on as Prime Minister for another year if I didn't say it".

It's thought that after these revelations Gordon Brown will be forced to stand down as Chancellor and take on the demeaning job of being Prime Minister.

Neasden Central Police Station

0900 hrs All leave cancelled to permit the entire Neasden force to attend an all-day training programme. This consisted of a showing of Episodes 1 to 12 of the BBC drama series 'Life On Mars'.

Officers were warned that they would find some scenes on the DVDs deeply disturbing, but they were instructed that the purpose of the presentation was to demonstrate how not to carry out policing duties in a modern social environment.

Officers were expected to take notes while the films were being shown, and to list all those incidents in which the police personnel were seen acting in an improper and inappropriate fashion.

After the showing, officers participated in a workshop session, at which they concluded that the most shocking failing of the police officer depicted in the training video was his repeated attempts to solve crimes and arrest criminals, rather than attending to more highly prioritised duties such as paperwork, internal equality monitoring and conducting health and safety assessments for officers likely to be exposed to a crime situation.

The following resolution was accordingly agreed: that, as a matter of the highest operational priority, an armed response unit should be deployed to arrest DCI Gene Hunt on 27 prima facie offences of bringing the police service into disrepute.

WANTED

Owing to the manpower deployment above, no police reserves were available to respond to a series of 999 calls reporting a "battle" in Primark Road between two alleged armed gangs comprising 381 young males of Somali origin, who were engaging in a "mass murdering incident".

"We're all in favour of cutting down packaging, but this is ridiculous..."

Local Election Special – 2am Edition
YES! IT'S MELTDOWN!

by Our Political Staff **Hugh Nose-Nothing**

MELTDOWN! That's the word we wrote down first before the results came in and that's the word we're sticking to as votes round the country show that in fact it wasn't really a meltdown at all.

But it certainly describes what's happening in the newsroom as all our forecasts fail to materialise and we begin to look a bit silly.

Wipe out! Landslide! Drubbing! Freefall! Yes, all these words have had to be replaced with something less dramatic as the British public showed exactly what they thought of pundits like us by creating a complex and rather boring voting pattern which didn't prove anything in particular except *(cont. p. 94)*

Those local election results in full

Middle England, South

Tristram Jolly-Goodbloke (OE), *Conservative*, 2704
Ron Himmler *BNP*, 1506
Gavin Windfarm, *Green*, 107
Jenny Organic-Sandal, *Lib Dem*, 32
Ted Busdriver, *Labour*, 0
Conservative gain

Cwm Dancing, Rhonda

Jones the Winner, *Plaid Cymru*, 2704
Jones the Loser, *Labour*, 1506
Jones the Lib Dem, *Lib Dem*, 107
Jones the Holiday Cottage on Fire, *Conservative*, 0
No change

Auchtermuchty, North

Glen Fiddich, *SNP,* 3742
Glen Morangie, *Lib Dem,* 4
Glen Elton, *Labour,* 3
Johnny Walker, *Conservative,* 0
Spoilt Ballots, 277,428
Carrier Pigeon votes expected next week (weather permitting)
SNP gain

Peter Mandelson admits New Labour indulged in too much spin

On other pages

☐ Bear admits to defecation in woods

☐ Pope admits to "Catholic tendencies"

The Daily Chain Mail

St Crispin's Day, The Year of Our Lord 1415   1 Groat

HARRY NOT TO GO TO AGINCOURT

by Lunchtime O'Bowsandarrows

THE British Army today ruled that it was "too dangerous" to send the young King Harry to fight at the battle of Agincourt.

The commanding officer General Bedford said that he had visited the site and declared that "the King would be an obvious target".

Knight Club

"With his distinctive armour and colourful Royal standard, he would attract the attention of French archers (Jeffroi d'Archole) and possibly endanger the troops around him."

The other Generals, Exeter, Warwick and Talbot, all agreed. "Harry might even be captured and held to ransom by the evil French," they said.

The King was said to be disappointed by the ruling, telling friends, "Once more unto the Boars Head, dear friends, once more".

INSIDE: Incredible Channel offer: Dover to Calais in only 14 hours!

Play I-Spy the MI5 Way

Agent One: *(Looking at photo of dodgy Islamist carrying bomb)* I spy with my little eye something beginning with T.
Agent Two: Terrorist?
Agent One: No Tea!
Agent Two: Excellent.

Agent One: Sugar?
Agent Two: I told you not to call me that in the office.
(Tea lady puts photo back in file)

New Miracle Face Cream from Boots

You'd never know I'm 107

HEATH

TEN YEARS OF BLAIR
Where Did The Analysis Go Wrong?

IT STARTED off so promisingly, as we all opened our 'Ten Years of Blair' supplements, full of anticipation and optimism. This was going to be good – new, fresh and exciting! But very soon our hopes were dashed and disillusion set in.

This was just the same old stuff rehashed. Not a radical different type of supplement at all. But the usual, cynical run-of-the-mill scissors and paste job that we had come to expect with profiles of John Major and Margaret Thatcher.

Spin... sleaze... cronies... we'd read it all before. And by the time it came to the Iraq War, we knew that the whole thing was all going to end disappointingly. Sadly, it would remain unfinished by most readers who (cont. p. 94)

NEXT WEEK
Special Supplement

"Will The Brown Years Usher In A Fresh Exciting New Era Of Something To Write About?"

"They'll never think of looking for illegal immigrants in here"

READ THE Daily Mail

–PICBROW–

TRIUMPH FOR BROWN AS HE DEFEATS NO ONE
by Our Political Staff **Peter O'Bore**

IN THE Labour Party's gripping leadership election, Gordon Brown romped home ahead of his rivals, of whom there were none.

In a thrilling finish, Brown fought off the non-existent challenge to pull off a result which everyone had predicted all along.

At Westminster, the news of Brown's landslide victory was greeted with gasps of boredom.

Said one insider, "It's really good to have a debate and to air the issues, which of course we didn't because everyone was too busy sucking up to Gordon in the hope of getting a job."

Right up to the last minute, the bookmakers were claiming that the race was "too close to call" and would "go right to the wire".

Gordon's odds of 3,000-1 on showed just how knife-edged the battle had become.

THOSE VOTES IN FULL

G. Brown 308
Nobody 0
No One 0
Others 0

*Brown gain.
Swing to Brown 100 percent*

WELL, what a surprise! MI5 has realised that women make better spies than men! This is not exactly news to those of us working mums whose job it is to know everything that's going on – from the secret location of their useless partner's missing sock to the Somalian for "You're fired, you silly girl, go back to what's left of your village!".

James Bond has got nothing on the average life-juggling über-mum: Ok, so he can drive an Aston Martin under water, but I can park a 4x4 in a disabled space right outside a North London prep school!

And maybe he can uncover the Mr Big who plans to take over the world, but I know who has been helping themselves to the chocolate biscuits in the cupboard (step forward Malnurishda from the Yemen – honestly, you would think on £1 a week, the greedy girl could buy her own?!).

SO what if 007 can turn off the death-ray machine that is going to blow up the world? I can turn off the Plasma TV when Simon is watching The World's Most Dangerous Trouser Presses with Richard Hammond on Sky Desperate Seven!

So, if 'M' is reading this, she(!) should know that if you want *intelligence*, then it's obvious that you recruit working women and not hopeless men !

Bond has a licence to kill! But Polly has a licence to fill (columns)!

The names Filler! Polly Filler!

© Polly Filler in all newspapers.

"Cheers!"

CHARLES NOT TO GO TO FRONT LINE
by Our Defence Staff **M. O'Dee**

THE QUEEN has decided that it would be too dangerous for her son Charles to be stationed in Buckingham Palace after her departure.

Although the Prince has made it clear that he wishes to take the post of King and serve his country "at the sharp end", the Queen believes that he would become a prime target for attacks

A royal insider said, "Snipers would have a field day as soon as Charles appeared. His silly dressing gown, his talking to plants and his wife jetting round the world creating a huge carbon footprint in the sky – it would all be too easy."

The Prince was last night said to be fuming at the Queen's decision to hold him back from where he feels his duty calls him to be.

"I didn't join the Royal Family just to sit on my arse back at Highgrove talking to tulips. It really is appalling."

Prince Charles is 94.

POETRY CORNER

In Memoriam
Terry Major-Ball

So. Farewell
Then Terry
Major-Ball.

Famous garden
Gnome manufacturer,
Author and
Larger-than-life
TV personality.

Keith says you
Had a brother
Who was once
A Prime Minister.

But you can't
Trust everything Keith
Says.

> E.J. Thribb (17½)

In Memoriam
Sir Malcolm Arnold,
famous composer

So. Farewell
Then Sir Malcolm
Arnold.

Famous composer
Of film and TV
Themes.

You won an
Oscar for
*Bridge On The
River Kwai.*

All together now –
Da da
Da da da
Dum-dum
Da
(Repeat).

Also farewell
Then
Chuck Rio
Saxophonist
And composer
Of *Tequila!*

Yes,
You were the man
Who shouted
"Tequila!"

All together now –
"Tequila!"

> E.J. Thribb (17½)

What You Missed

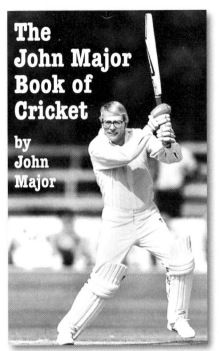

The John Major Book of Cricket by John Major

CHAPTER ONE
A Very English Game

EVER since I was a boy I have been not inconsider-ably interested in cricket. Oh yes. In my judgement it is probably the most interesting game there is. As I said to my wife Norman this morning (obviously when this book is published it will be not inconsiderably later than this morning that I said it!), "There is something about cricket which makes it particularly interesting".

CHAPTER TWO
How I First Became Interested In Cricket

I FIRST became interested in cricket when I was quite young. I still remember the day when my older brother Terry went with me to choose my very first bat at Whiteleafs (not Disdale's, as Terry recorded wrongly in his book).

It was a "Jack Hobbs Three Star Special", named after a famous cricketer called Jack Hobbs, who played for Surrey, which was where I lived! Oh yes.

The bat had Mr Hobbs's signature on it, although it was not his real signature, as Terry took no small pleasure in telling me at repeated intervals.

In my judgement it was an extremely fine bat, and I wish I still had it.

I was not inconsiderably incandescent with rage when, many years later, I went to the attic to look for it and found it was no longer there because my wife Norman had given it to a bring-and-buy sale.

CHAPTER THREE
My First Visit To The Oval

I WILL never forget my first visit to the Oval, to see one of the great players of all time, Mr Cyril Washbrook, who many years later I was privileged to recommend for an honour to Her Majesty The Queen. It was a CBE which, as I rather humorously pointed out to my wife Norman, could stand for "Cyril Batted for England". "Isn't there an 'F' missing?", she asked, clearly failing to see the joke.

Sometimes women are not very good at cricket, or jokes for that matter!

After the match, in which Mr Washbrook made 31 before being caught at mid-off by Mr

Sir Alec Bedser (or it may have been his twin brother Eric, it was difficult to tell them apart because they were twins!), we called our pet squirrel after Mr Washbrook, which is why he was known as 'Cyril the Squirrel' (and not 'Basil the Squirrel', as Terry claimed in his in no small measure poorly-researched book!).

CHAPTER FOUR
Cricket And My Years At Number 10 Downing Street

ONE of the things I most considerably regretted when I had the great privilege to become prime minister was that I did not have sufficient leisure time to pursue my interest in cricket.

I once invited the famous French President Mr Monsieur Mitterand to accompany me to Lords to watch a test match, but he replied "non", which in my judgement was not inconsiderably rude of him!

CHAPTER FIVE
The Final Score

IN conclusion, I would like to conclude by saying that cricket has for many centuries been part and parcel of our English way of life. Oh yes, we think of cricket along with old maids drinking warm beer on their way to Communion in the fog... Neat rows of red and white traffic cones along our highways and byways... Love romps with Mrs Curry in the afternoon... (Who put this bit in? It has nothing to do with cricket whatsoever. I told the publishers that I did not want any mention of Mrs Curry in a book about cricket, but they have gone against my wishes, which makes me not inconsiderably very angry in no small measure indeed!)

● Listen to John Major reading extracts from his book on the new exclusive Eye podcast.

Daily Mail
FRIDAY, APRIL 27, 2007

WILL SOARING HOUSE PRICES LEAD TO COLLAPSE IN HOUSE PRICES?

By Our Entire Staff
Paul Filthy-Dacre

THERE was widespread panic all across Middle England today as it was announced that house prices have risen by 84 percent since I started writing this piece.

Experts were warning that this could precipitate a catastrophic collapse in house prices by as much as 84 percent by the time I have reached the end of this article.

On other pages: *Can Cancer Give You Cancer?* A Mail Health Special.

*"Old hotels and old beds always have lots of creepy-crawlies, but **this** bed seems to be free of bed-bugs at least"*

Fayed v. Sanity (Day 94)

Before Mrs Justice Slosslecarrot

(The interlocutory proceedings continued today, as Counsel for Mr Fugger presented a list of witnesses he intended to call before the court)

Michael Largecheque Q.C. *(for Mr al-Fugger)*: I beg leave, My Lord Ladyship, to submit the names of the 758 witnesses whom my client, in all his lunacy, would wish to call, for no apparent reason. You will find the list in Bundle 94.

Judge Butler-Slosslecarrot: Mr Largecheque, I am having some difficulty finding the exact bundle of documents to which you refer. Is it in the first container-load, which hereinafter I shall refer to as 'Container A', or the second lorry-load, parked on a double yellow line in the Strand, which hereafter this court will refer to as 'B'?

Mr al-Fugger *(interrupting)*: I thought we'd got rid of this fuggin' old bag?

Judge Slosslecarrot: Kindly sit down, Mr Fugger, while I pursue my searches.

Largecheque: Would it help to expedite proceedings, Your Ladyship, if I was to read out the names in question?

Judge: I am indebted to you, Mr Largecheque.

Largecheque: And I am indebted to my client Mr Fugger for the third container-load full of money, hereinafter referred to as 'Container C', which he has given me in order to ensure that we can spin out proceedings for as long as possible, or what we lawyers call *in re perpetua*.

Fugger *(interrupting again)*: Speak fuggin' English, Largecheque, that's what I pay you for.

Judge: Mr Fugger, I will not warn you again. Any more interruptions of this nature and I will have to ask you to leave the court.

Fugger: I'm fuggin' sorry, Your Fuggin' Lordship.

Judge: Can we please return to the matter of the list? Who are these names that your client wishes to call, Mr Largecheque?

Largecheque: Indeed, Your Honour. I am happy to oblige. *(Reading)* "Mr Dirty Desmond, proprietor of the *Daily Express* newspaper. Mr Piers Moron, a very distinguished celebrity and friend of my client. Professor Uri Geller, Reader in Spoonistics at the University of the Paranormal, Uruguay. His Holiness the Pope. Dame Eliza Manningham-Butler, the former head of MI5. Commander James Bond, RN, late of MI6. Sir Roland Rat, the former Director-General of the BBC. The Chief Rabbi. The Chief Dalek. The late Rudolf Hess."

Judge: This list of yours is preposterous! You will be telling me next that you wish to call Her Majesty the Queen!

Largecheque: What uncanny prescience, Your Ladyship! Her Majesty's name is the very next one on the list. It is my client's contention that she lies at the very heart of this murky affair. You will hear new evidence that the Queen persuaded Mr Paul Burrell, the Royal butler, to drive a white Fiat Uno into that fateful tunnel on the night in question, thus engineering the fatal crash which had been so carefully planned by His Royal Highness the Duke of Edinburgh, the counter-espionage organisation SMERSH, and Mr Darth Vader, in his capacity as Supreme Commander of the Imperial Forces on the Death Star Battleship Galactica.

Judge: Mr Largecheque, these are indeed somewhat controversial allegations which will require me to spend some time lying down in a darkened room, before I happily hand over this case to somebody else.

(The case continues)

I.T. SYSTEM DOESN'T CRASH

A GOVERNMENT department was forced to apologise last night after its new I.T. system didn't crash.

"We simply cannot understand what went right here: we followed all the usual procedures used by the Registry Office, the NHS and the DSS; the project was hopelessly mismanaged from the start, millions over budget and delivered ten years late," said the civil servant in charge.

"And yet when we switched it on, instead of everyone's personal records being erased or put on public view, the new system started working perfectly.

"We're pretty confident that this was just a one-off, and that by Monday we'll be in the same mess as every other government department."

CHANNEL 4 DOCUMENTARY OUTRAGE
Why can't Diana be given privacy in her death?

ON OTHER PAGES

YES IT'S BRYAN FÜHRERRY!

© *Reichsy Musik — Greatest Hitlers*

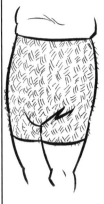
What Name Do You Think the Ex-Spice Girl Baby Should Have Been Given?

You choose from the following showbiz alternatives:

① Sunblest Aerosol
② Lemon Fresh Weetabix
③ Grapefruit Segment Dettol
④ Sir Peregrine Worsthorne
⑤ Full English Breakfast
⑥ Bluebell Madonna Halliwell

WARNING: This poem may be adversely affected by late election results due to voting irregularities and an investigation by the Electoral Commission

Lines Written On The Breakup Of The Anglo-Scottish Union After 300 Historic Years

BY WILLIAM REES-MCGONAGALL

'Twas in the year two thousand and seven
That Scottish folk everywhere believed they were in heaven.
By voting in their millions for the SNP,
They believed that at last Caledonia had been set free.

For 'twas back in the reign of Bonnie Queen Anne
That all this sorry business first began.
When the proud Scots submitted to the Sassenach yoke,
Which I assure you was very far frae being a joke.

For three hundred years despite their bravery,
Yon puir Scots had to endure a life of slavery.
In misery they had to sweat and toil
While the English came in to plunder their oil.

And throughout all this long and dismal time
The wicked English committed against the Scots every kind of crime.
They even removed the historic Stone of Scone
And put it in a prominent place in London toon.

But then after nearly three centuries of shame,
The long-awaited day of reckoning came.
The English thought a devolved Parliament would be a solution,
But instead they sparked a Tartan revolution.

From Gretna Green to John O'Groats,
The Scottish nation cast its votes.
From the highlands to the lowlands, from far and wide,
They placed their crosses Alex Salmond's name beside.

But was this a vote for Scottish independence?,
Or more that they wished to pass on Mr Blair a death sentence?
Did they want to get their country back?
Or just punish Blair for invading Iraq?

Och aye, the Scots ended up parting from their neighbour,
Because they could no longer bring themselves to vote Labour,
So Mr Salmond became Braveheart's heir
Just because everyone in Scotland hated Blair.

© W. Rees-McGonagall.

● Do you agree with the above poem? Or do you think there were other reasons for the swing to the Scottish National Party? Or maybe you're Welsh and you don't care? Or perhaps you're angry that the above poem isn't about the elections for the Welsh Assembly? Why don't you join the debate by logging on to www.fillupelectionissueoverquietbankholidayweekend.com?

"You could at least put him out in the garden"

SAVE THE PLANET

PRIVATE EYE COMPETITION

How green are you?

Simply answer these nine questions to see how your lifestyle is helping to save Planet Earth from the total disaster of global warming in less than ten years' time.

1 How much of your bathwater do you recycle in cups of fairtrade tea each week?
(a) one litre
(b) 12 cubic metres
(c) 38 organic hectares

2 Do you fill your bicycle tyres
(a) half full?
(b) quarter full?
(c) No, I walk everywhere.

3 What do you do with your carbon-intensive plastic bags? Do you
(a) put them in the compost heap?
(b) recycle them as carriers for other plastic bags?
(c) I have a string bag, actually.

4 Before going to bed at night, do you switch off
(a) your television?
(b) your computer?
(c) Everything, including our fridge.

5 As your main energy source, does your home have
(a) a megawatt wind turbine?
(b) a solar-panelled roof?
(c) We have given up using electricity, thank you, and use only organic candles.

6 Which of the following have you stopped eating?
(a) meat
(b) carbon-intensive barley sugar
(c) Everything – we're fasting, thank you very much.

7 Are your shoes made of
(a) carbon-intensive plastic?
(b) GM leather?
(c) Clogs made from recycled tyres from the Third World, since you're asking.

8 Is your roof insulated with
(a) Tibetan yaks' wool?
(b) old copies of the Guardian containing pieces by George Monbiot?
(c) We live in a tent, so there!

9 Every year you breathe in oxygen and breathe out 5,914 tons of deadly, polluting carbon dioxide. Should you
(a) plant a 200-acre forest of mixed deciduous trees in your back garden?
(b) carry a cylinder to 'capture' the CO2 so that you can bury it under your patio?
(c) We've stopped breathing, actually.

Dans le European Summit

Monsieur Sarkozy (*pour c'est lui*): Bonjour Tony. Ici un treaty très important that Herr Merkel a composé.

Monsieur Blair: Qu'est-ce que c'est dans le treaty!

Madame Merkel: Ne worry pas! Ce n'est pas dodgy comme certain dossiers je could mention!

Blair: Mais it's not a constitution j'espère.

Sarkozy: Ooh la la. Non!

Merkel: Constitution? Quelle Horreure!?

Sarkozy: Ok. Juste un bit – mais considerez this a moment!

Blair: Que?

Sarkozy: If cette dossier non-dodgy *were* un constitution...

Merkel: Which it is *nein*..

Sarkozy: Toute la Power would go to le nouveau President – le grand fromage, le banana en haut...

Merkel: Le Führer...

Blair: Et qui sera le nouveau President!

Sarkozy: Vous mon ami!!!!! Vous êtes le first choice!

Blair: Donnez moi la plume! Où do I sign?!!

NEXT WEEK: Le pauvre Gordon realises que Tony est his new boss!?

© *Kilometres Kington*

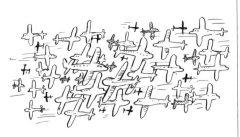

"We need some 'blue sky thinking' on this"

ST CAKES HEAD DEFENDS SELECTION ON ABILITY

by Our Educational Staff **G.C.S.E. Fayle**

MR R.J. Kipling (M.A.), headmaster of St Cakes, the prestigious Midlands independent school for boys, last night joined the heated debate about the future of education in Britain.

Said Mr Kipling: "There is nothing wrong with selection on ability providing it is the ability to pay enormous fees.

"Here at St Cakes," he continued, "we are not ashamed of the rigorous entry exam which we require pupils to pass. We call it the 11-Grand-Plus Test and we demand that boys should be able to give me a cheque for at least £11,000 every term.

"We find that this ensures that St Cakes has a very high class intake of money and only the highest standards of payment are admitted."

Means Testing

The headmaster pointed to the success of his policy in terms of the league tables where St Cakes this year appears just above Monaco in terms of GDP.

Mr Kipling concluded, "If I let in boys from poorer backgrounds then I would obviously find that the quality of my car would be affected – not to mention the standard of my holidays."

The St Cakes motto is "Demonstrando Me Argentum" ("Show Me The Money").

THE BOOK OF EHUD

Chapter 94: The Miracle in Gaza

1. And lo, it came to pass in the land that is called Gaza, that the Hamasites rose up against the Fatahites.

2. And the Hamasites cried out, "The Fatahites have failed to lead the sons of Palestine to their chosen land or rather the land chosen for them by the children of Israel.

3. "It is time for the Hamasites to sit in the thrones of power even as the Palestinianites have chosen (well, not all of them, obviously)."

4. And the Palestinianites took arms one against the other and the Hamasites smote the Fatahites.

5. And the Fatahites smote the Hamasites.

6. And there was much wailing and gnashing of teeth.

7. And the blood runneth like unto an river in the city that is called Gaza City.

8. And when Ehud, the leader of the Israelites, heard of this he rejoiceth.

9. For verily he could not believeth his luck. For he saith, "Verily it is like unto two scorpions in the sand who stingeth each other even unto death – instead of stinging the man with the big flip-flop who walketh on the beaches of Eilat.

10. "Even thus the Hamasites and Fatahites will smite one another an hundredfold and the burden of smiting will be lifted from the children of Israel."

11. And he gave thanks to God, saying, "Yea, it is a miracle. Your servant Ehud is thrice blessed".

12. But the Lord spake unto him, "Counteth not thy chickens, matey, before they are hatched. For this one will endeth badly. Marketh my words".

To be continued...

"Oh no, insurge-ants!"

'WOOLMER NOT ALIVE'

Jamaican Police New Claim

by Our Man In The West Indies **Trevor Barbados**

IN THE latest sensational twist to the mystery surrounding the death of the Pakistani cricket coach Bob Woolmer, the head of the Jamaican police investigation Inspector 'Knacker of the Yardie' Knacker yesterday held a press conference to announce that his enquiries were now concluded.

"I know I said in earlier reports that Mr Woolmer had been strangled by the entire Pakistani team, poisoned by 'match fixers' from the sub-continent, eaten by Dr No-style crocodiles, or was possibly alive and well and living happily with Shergar and the late Lord Lucan somewhere in Mozambique" said the Inspector.

"I now realise that he died of natural causes, that there were no suspicious circumstances surrounding his death and that you may find it difficult to take anything I say seriously *(cont. p 94)*

● Do you have a theory about the fate of Bob Woolmer? Do you have no qualifications to talk about this at all? Then we'd like to hear from you, and your views will be given equal prominence with those of Simon Heffer on our new Read-It-On-The-Blog page at www. desperateforrubbish.telegraph.co.uk

Nursery Times

Friday, April 27, 2007

DYKE WHITTINGTON SAYS NO

by Our London Staff **Walter de la Mayor**

MR DYKE Whittington shocked Nurseryland yesterday by refusing to "turn again" and become Mayor, going home instead.

Dyke had set out with his faithful rat, Roland, to seek fame and fortune in London whose pavements he had been told were paved with crap (surely gold? Ed.).

Along the way he met a strange young man called Dave who promised him that he could be Mayor of London. All he had to do was defeat the evil Red Ken and his trusty newt.

Puss-In-Newts

Dyke, however, took one look at the silky-tongued old Etonian in his cycling helmet and told him, "Cut the crap. You must be joking. I've got loadsamoney, what do I want a headache for, etc. etc."

Whereupon Dyke turned upon his heels and the bells of London cried out:

*Phew that was close
He's already dumbed down
                    the BBC
And London's dumb
enough
                    as it is.*
(Is this right? Ed.)

On other pages

Cinderella too common for Prince Charming, claim courtiers. She said "shoe" instead of "slipper" **94**

71

IRAQ

'Things are getting better'

writes MoD spokesman **Mike Toady**

HAVING recently returned from Iraq, I can tell you that, contrary to endless whingeing reports from the likes of Sir Max Hastings and the rest of the anti-war brigade, large areas of the country are entirely quiet and peaceful.

These places, known locally as 'deserts', are largely populated by sand.

I can assure you that everyday life in these regions of Iraq is much the same as it has always been. No terrorism, no suicide bombers, no insurgents, indeed no people at all.

This gives the lie to (cont. p. 94)

THE ALTERNATIVE VOICE

DAVE SPART (Co-Chair of the Troops Out of Iran and Free The Guacamole Bay Three Now campaign) writes on the 150th anniversary of the birth of Sir Edward Elgar.

It is totally sickening the way the media, ie the capitalist press and the state-run puppet regime at the BBC, have shamelessly promulgated non-stop tributes to the arch-reactionary Edward Elgar, the imperialist lackey who composed such notorious jingoistic tunes as the *Land of Pomp and Circumstance* and other Fascist marching songs that whipped up the hysteria that directly resulted in the First World War and the deaths of millions of innocent Germans at the hands of the hated British-American Coalition forces who had invaded Europe on the totally spurious pretext that the Kaiser Wilhelm had weapons of mass destruction, ie poison gas, when all along the ulterior motive was to get their greedy hands on German oil, er, a conspiracy to which Elgar gave his 100 percent support by writing his cello concerto.

● *Do you agree with Dave Spart that Elgar should be tried as a war criminal, along with Milosevic, Rumsfeld and Blair? Or would you prefer to listen to Sir Arnold Bax's tone-poem* Tintagel*? We don't care, but the editor's desperate to fill the paper, so please write something, even if it's only what you had for breakfast, at www.morerubbishnow.allpapers.co.uk*

Magnificent 2007

"We are poor farmers, we wish to hire a website designer to highlight the trouble our village has with bandits..."

"He doesn't like to talk about it now, but Frank was in the Falklands..."

THE ⁂ TIMES

Friday March 20 2028

25th Anniversary of War Commemorated

by Our Defence Staff **Stanley Port and Georgia South**

Yes, it was 25 years ago today that our boys went into Iraq to liberate Baghdad after it wasn't invaded. And yet nearly a quarter of a century later we are still there. Who would have thought it?

The occasion was marked by no celebrations, no services and the traditional protest march past, demanding "Troops Out Now".

Don't Rejoice!

It seems like only yesterday that there was fierce fighting on the other side of the world and heavy casualties for the stretched British Armed Forces – that's because it was only yesterday.

'WE ARE THE REAL HEIRS TO BLAIR' — Tories claim

by Our Political Staff **Peter O'Bore**

IN a savage attack on the Conservative Party, David Cameron last night pledged that he and his followers were the real successors to New Labour.

"It's obvious," he said, "that the most successful politician of modern times is Tony Blair and that the only way to succeed is to be as much like him as possible".

Tory Blair

"The first thing about Tony," Mr Cameron continued, "is that he came to power because he wasn't a Conservative. So it makes sense for us not to be Conservatives either! That's the way you win elections!"

Cameron's colleague George Osborne was quick to pick up the theme. "Gordon Brown isn't very like Tony. No way! But we are! That's why we're going to win."

And David Willetts, known as the brains of the Cameron team, spelled out what this meant in terms of policy.

Bad Grammar

"Tories are in favour of grammar schools," he said. "That's why it is very important that we should be against them.

"The same applies to our thinking right across the board. Tories want low taxes – we want them going up. Tories want law and order – we're against it. Tories believe in marriage – we say ban it!"

LATE NEWS
● **Poll shock – Cameron now "as unpopular as Blair".**

A Taxi Driver writes

Every week a well-known taxi driver writes on an issue of topical importance. This week **Jimmy 'Doc' Reid**, Glasgow Cab No. 666, on the problem of reoffending paedophiles.

D'you see about these paedos, McGuv, you know what I'd do with them? Cut their balls off. And I tell you what, McGuv, a lot of them would thank you for it! Tell you something else, they're everywhere. Could be one living right next to you. There could be one in the back of my cab now. In fact, you could be one yourself. I'm not taking you anywhere with your filthy habits. Get out, you pervert, before I cut them off!

NEXT WEEK: Sid Snotter (Cab No. 2012) on the shortcomings in the design of the logo for the London Olympics, and the likelihood that his four-year-old son Dwayne could have produced a more acceptable image with his eyes closed.

God Is Not Great
(But Bush is Marvellous!)

 by Christopher Hitchens

MANY stupid people refuse to believe in a supreme power. I felt like that once but then I had a moment of revelation when I realised that everyone was talking nonsense and that there was an all-powerful benign intelligence that controlled our destinies.

Seen the Light

The ignorant and the uneducated blamed Him for allowing wars in which thousands died or floods in which people's homes were swept away while He merely looked on.

"Why does He allow evil to happen?" they asked, as if this was a sensible question. But it isn't. The fact remains that George Bush *does* exist. Although He moves in mysterious ways and His sayings are sometimes difficult to comprehend, if we have faith in George Bush all will be revealed and our lives will be transformed. We could not wish for more.

● Christopher Hitchens will be getting drunk in Tent 94 at the Hay-on-Wye festival. If you want a signed copy of Richard Dawkins' book on God, he is in Tent 666.

CHESS NEWS

"Ah! The Bush defence"

That completely different EU Treaty that we don't need to have a referendum about
TEXT IN FULL

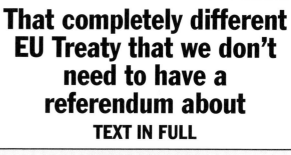

A ~~Constitution~~ Reform Treaty For The European Union

❶ There shall be a full-time President ~~of~~ for the EU.

❷ The EU shall have its own ~~Foreign Minister~~ High Representative.

❸ Nation states shall lose their right of veto over ~~all~~ most matters.

❹ The EU can do whatever it wants whenever it chooses, including ignoring the previous three articles.

❺ The rest of the ~~Constitution~~ Treaty shall remain the same *(take in remaining 900 pages of original text)*.

❻ Mrs Merkel to buy lunch for everyone as a reward for their ~~conniving in~~ agreeing to this ~~appalling deception~~ brilliant diplomatic triumph.

The Daily Telegraph

Friday, June 22, 2007

GCSE Joy Sweeps Nation

by Our Education Staff
Phil Homework-Folder

THERE were scenes of jubilation at schools across the nation as delighted parents received the result they were hoping for – that GCSE coursework is to be scrapped.

"I'm thrilled," said one teenager's dad. "It's just what I was hoping for," said another youngster's mother. "Now I don't have to write any more essays or do any more projects ever again!"

But there was

dismay among traditionalists about the effect this would have on standards. Said a 16-year-old expert, "This is bound to lead to a

decline in the quality of my leisure time. How on earth am I supposed to watch television if my parents are not going to *(cont. p. 94)*

WIMBLEDON SIX TO WATCH

🎾 An Eye Cut-out-'n'-keep Guide To 🎾
The Greatest Tennis Tournament in the World

Strato cumulus

Top-rated rain cloud with consistent Wimbledon form. Excellent on grass.

Cumulo nimbus

Delivers powerful rain which should guarantee a second week showing at the home of rain.

Nimbo stratus

A dark cloud *(surely "horse")* which some experts reckon has the ability to make it to the final and ruin everything.

——— *That's enough clouds. Ed.* ———

QUEEN – THE MUSICAL

♪ I'm ♪
reigning in
the rain

'I WAS THERE AS THE LAST CIGARETTE WAS STUBBED OUT'

by **Lunchtime O'Boozebutnofags**

YES! I was there as a thousand-year-old British tradition finally came to an end in the smoke-filled snug of the Blackberry & Laptop (formerly The Lamb & Flag) in London's Fenchurch Street.

Here, along with dozens of die-hard smokers, I was determined to savour my nicotine pleasure for the last time before the bell struck midnight and the heavy hand of the nanny state ordered us all to "Put that fag out!".

I have to admit there was a tear in my eye because of the smoke and a lump in my throat because I've got cancer.

Why oh why have they betrayed all of us who fought in two world wars for the right to *(cont. p. 94)*

Parents: how to turn your teens off smoking for life

That Honorary Degree Citation In Full

SALUTAMUS YUSUFUM ISLAMICUM QUONDAM FELIX STEVENENSIS POPULARE CANTORUM FAMOSSISSIMUM 'MATUTINUS FRAGMENTUS EST' 'MATTEUS FILIUSQUE' 'AMO CANEM MEUM' ET MULTOS ALTEROS SIMILAROS SED CONVERTUS AD RELIGIONI ISLAMICO CUM BARBO LONGO ET VESTIBUS ARABICIS MUSICO NUNC PROHIBITUS SILENTOGUITARIPERMULTOSANNOSGAUDEAMUS LAUDATE ALLAM.

THE PRINCE OF GREENS

THE STORY SO FAR... Charles is delighted by his success at running an organic vegetable business. But is all as well as it seems?

A STEADY June drizzle was falling on the celebrated Stuart Rose Garden at Highgrove.

Inside, Charles sat in the breakfast room, leafing through the pile of letters that had just been brought in by his faithful valet, Faucet, on a silver tray.

The Prince's face flushed with pleasure as he read a fulsome thank-you letter from the Auchtermuchty General Stores near Balmoral, informing him that they had just sold a record three packets of his Duchy Beetroot and Rhubarb Chocolate Hob-Nobs, only one of which had been returned by the customer.

And then there was a letter from the Chief Druid inviting him, in his role as Defender of All Faiths, to say a few words at Stonehenge during their next celebration of the Summer Solstice.

But what was this? A letter from Sainsbury's, no doubt congratulating him on the quality of his new Duchy range of organic vegetables, which had just appeared on the shelves of their supermarkets.

Wasn't this the greatest tribute that had ever been paid to his skills as an organic businessman and royal horticulturalist?

A beaming Charles slipped his ivory paper knife (a memento of an historic elephant shoot at Simla in 1903 by his great-great-grandfather Edward VII) into the envelope bearing the legend *"Sainsbury's – It All Tastes The Same"*.

But, as he read the text of the letter within, his face darkened and he furiously brought down his silver spoon on the hapless head of boiled egg No. 5.

"What's the matter, darling?" cried Camilla from across the table, as she lifted her eyes from the Easy Sudoku on the Coffee Break pages of the Daily Mail.

She had not seen her husband looking so distressed since the theft of his Mitchell & Webb watercolour set outside Cairo, when he was still only half-way through his study of the Pyramids By Moonlight.

"Listen to this, Cazza. It really is, well..." he thought long and hard, but the word wouldn't come. "Never mind." It was whatever it was and he began to read out to Camilla the letter which had caused him such visible distress.

"Dear Sir or Madam," it began. *"Re your delivery of organic carrots of the 16th,*

A romantic summer read from the pen of Dame Sylvie Krin, author of La Dame Aux Camillas, Duchess of Hearts, Heir of Sorrows and hundreds more.

we must inform you that, following an inspection by our Quality Control team, the deficiencies in your product were noted as below:

1. The carrots failed to comply with our firm's rigorous Wrinkle Standard. 17 of the 23 carrots tested were excessively wrinkled and would be perceived by our customers as too old to be fit for purpose.

2. There was some evidence of penetration of the carrots by root weevil, rendering the carrots limp and unsightly.

At this point, Camilla loyally interjected, "What a bloody nerve, Chazza!"

"No. There's worse to come," said Charles, reading on.

"In the view of our controllers, these carrots have been left in the ground too long. They are well past their prime and simply not good enough. Yours faithfully, M. Bovis, Area Purchasing Manager for Organic Vegetables and Barbecue Equipment, South-West Region (North)."

Charles hurled the offending missive across the table, where it landed in the remains of Camilla's Full English Breakfst, brought in from Ken's Mobile Breakfast Bar on the A46 Stroud lay-by.

Camilla rose and placed a soothing hand on her husband's shoulder, saying, "No wonder you're upset, Chazza. Why don't you go and have a lie down? Who does this little man think he is, talking to you like that about your wonderful carrots? It's simply not good enough..."

"SIMPLY not good enough." Charles inexplicably found himself lying prostrate on a cold, metal supermarket shelf.

An enormous woman in a white coat was looking severely down at him, prodding him with her finger.

"This one won't do. Too old, wrinkled, limp... and look at all these holes."

Come to think of it, thought Charles, the woman looked uncannily like the mater, Her Majesty the Queen.

And why was she working in a supermarket with a crown on her head? It didn't make any sort of sense. And why was he so small?

"Been in the ground too long!" barked a male voice in the background. "Weevils have got at him. Punters will never go for something looking like this."

Charles knew that voice! It was Pater, the Duke of Edinburgh, wearing a plastic badge on his white coat identifying him as "Phil Windsor, Vegetable Quality Control Supervisor".

Charles tried to respond from his recumbent position on the shelf. But it seemed the two giant figures could not hear him.

"I don't go for all this organic nonsense," growled the big man, as he put a huge cross in the "Quality Rating" box on the form on his clipboard.

"Just because it's covered in mud doesn't mean that it's any bloody good. We should chuck it out right away."

The giant hand reached out to Charles, who screamed in terror.

"You don't understand, you don't understand..."

"YOU don't understand..." Charles woke up with a start to find Camilla leaning over him looking concerned. "It's alright, darling," she said comfortingly. "You must have been having some horrid dream."

"Yes," he said, "it was really, you know..."

"What, darling?" she prompted.

"I can't think of the word," he replied, rubbing his eyes and walking over to the window for a breath of fresh air.

But, as he looked out, he saw a huge 40-tonne truck inscribed with the slogan *"Sainsbury's – Taste No Difference"*, backing up to the edge of the lawn, and disgorging a mighty cascade of rotting carrots all over his prize rose beds.

At last he remembered the word he had been trying to think of earlier. "Appalling." That was it. There was no other word for it.

© Sylvie Krin 2007.

Nation Mourns 'The People's Prime Minister'

by Our Entire Staff

FROM early yesterday, the streets of London were lined with vast crowds drawn from all over the nation, weeping openly as they mourned the passing of the man they called simply "Princess Tony".

Every pavement was piled high with flowers wrapped in cellophane, many bearing such touching handwritten messages as "We shall always love you, Tony", "The world will be empty without you" and "God forgive Gordon for killing you, we never will".

By midday the police had erected crash barriers all down the Mall, as millions besieged Buckingham Palace, angrily demanding that the Queen reinstate Tony as their rightful king.

Premier of Hearts

Millions queued patiently for several minutes to sign books of condolence, while in St Paul's Cathedral, the Archbishop of Canterbury led a service of thanksgiving for the life of the man he described as "the nearest thing to a saint we shall ever see on this earth".

A highlight of the service was the world premier of a new "tribute song" by Sir Elton John entitled "Crocodile Tears Rock".

Never Glad Confident Mourning Again

As Big Ben chimed midnight, the entire nation was still trying to come to terms with their loss and, for some, grief was turning into something uglier.

"I blame the media," said one father of four, who gave his name only as T. Blair. "They hounded him out of office, especially the Independent. Bastards, going on about Iraq all the time when we'd drawn a line under it long ago.

"Make no mistake," he went on, "he was the best prime minister we've ever had. We shall never see my like again."

● Did you weep when you heard the news that Tony Blair had been forced out of office? Or were you watching the tennis? Or were you trying to clear the floodwater out of your living room? Anyway, whatever, we'd like to hear from you! Send us up to 1,000 words on any subject you like and, no matter how boring, we'll put it in our new 'Read It On The Blog' page. Just text or email your message to www. desperatetelegraphrubbish. co.uk.

"Okay, Gordon, you can be leader now"

10 YEARS OF RORY

TONY BLAIR looks back at the Bremner years and highlights the successes and failures of Britain's longest-serving TV impressionist. How will he be remembered?

Blair wonders whether Rory's undoubted talents will be eclipsed by his fatal error of taking himself far too seriously. The Prime Minister assesses Bremner's position in history and discusses his long-term legacy with such luminaries as Mike Yarwood.

CABINET WHIP ROUND FOR BLAIR'S LEAVING PRESENT

We've raised £1700

That won't even get me a peerage

Mary Ann Bighead

Goodbye to Blair – but more importantly to me!

You will be sad to hear that this is my final Bighead column in the Times. From now on I'm going to be a roving Bighead, penning a few clever pieces, writing a very clever book and doing the odd spot of extremely clever broadcasting.

It's what I call rather cleverly a portfolio existence. And of course I'll be spending more time with my children Brainella (7) and Intelligencia (3) as they go to university and complete their PhDs in Advanced Cleverology.

But as I leave I know the thing I shall miss most is *you* – the readers who have constantly surprised me by being clever enough to understand my articles. It's not an easy read, the Bighead column, but from my postbag it's quite clear that a few of you are almost as clever as me! So farewell – or, as they say in journalism, "Please, please, please take voluntary redundancy, Mary Ann."

© Blairy Ann Bighead

IN   IN!!!

Farewell to the King of the Chat Shows

by Our Showbiz Staff

Tony welcomes Parky onto his show

THE WORLD of television will never be the same again. In his long and distinguished career, he met everyone who was anyone and his irresistible cocktail of wit and charm captivated them all, from pop singer to Popes, from top Hollywood star to sporting legends.

The master of small-talk welcomed them onto his famous sofa and had his picture taken with them all.

None of us will ever remember what was said during his encounters with David Beckham, the Dalai Lama, Arnold Schwarzenegger, Nelson Mandela, Andy Flintoff, Bob Geldof, the Pope and the Spice Girls.

But the one incident which no one will forget was the wonderfully embarrassing encounter with the puppeteer George Bush, who treated his host as though he were a pet emu.

From the moment he greeted him with the derisive words "Yo, Blair", the smooth frontman of 1000 TV interviews knew that this time it was all going to go horribly wrong.

He tried to turn off the microphone in a desperate bid to save his dignity. But the damage was already done and only a few months later he had to resign.

In his retirement, Blairky plans to write his memoirs, listing all the famous people he has met during his dazzling, celebrity-filled career.

FLOODS OVERWHELM CENTRAL LONDON

WESTMINSTER yesterday became the latest victim of the extreme weather conditions currently affecting most areas of the British Isles.

In dramatic scenes in the House of Commons over six hundred people were nearly drowned as floods of tears rose to almost shoulder level.

One eye-witness told reporters, "We feared for our lives as the water level kept rising every time the Prime Minister opened his mouth."

Said another, "It's a miracle we are still alive. One minute it was an ordinary Prime Minister's

Question Time and we were happily asleep.

"But then Margaret Beckett began to sniffle and Patricia Hewitt welled up and suddenly the floodgates opened and the weeping began. In no time at all the water was lapping around our waists."
● Full report and pictures: **pp 3,4,5,6,94**.

GOODBYE BLAIR

THAT ALL-CHANGE BROWN CABINET IN FULL

by Peter O'Bore

YES, it's the biggest reshuffle in the history of British politics as Gordon Brown unveils his glittering cabinet of all the talents.

OUT GOES Jack Straw, 69, the failed Foreign Secretary and Leader of the House.

IN COMES Jack Straw, 47, dynamic high flier who will take over the new-look Ministry of Justice.

OUT GOES Des Browne, 73, discredited Defence Secretary blamed for Iraq fiasco.

IN COMES Des Browne, 39, charismatic new Defence Secretary who will sort out the fiasco in Iraq.

OUT GOES Ruth Kelly, 42, ineffectual former Education Secretary and the minister widely blamed for the Housing Information Pack disaster.

IN COMES Ruth Kelly, 37, feisty, brilliant, trouser-suited member of Opus Dei. Charged with bringing a halt to Britain's transport. *(Is this right? Ed.)*

OUT GOES Hazel Blears, Alistair Darling, Geoff Hoon, Hilary Benn etc., etc.

IN COMES Hazel Blears, Alistair Darling, Geoff Hoon, Hilary Benn etc., etc.

THE OUTSIDERS

Brown has promised a Government that will look outside the traditional career structure to recruit the very best of British talent to bring a new-look to the whole process of decision making.

Inspector Knacker of the Yard. The 81-year-old former Metropolitan Police Chief is known to shoot from the hip even if he often gets the wrong man.

Admiral Sir Alan Pugwash. Falklands Naval hero who led a daring attack on Tony Blair *(Surely Port Stanley? Ed.)*

Sir Digby Redface, 72. Former CBI chief whose motto "Sod the workers" has endeared him to the new-look Labour party.

Dame Shirley Temple, 99. Former LibDem MP tap dancer and member of the Crazy Gang of Four, Dame Shirley has been given the brief of annoying Ming Cambell, 107.

INTRODUCING THE MILIBAND TWINS

Ted or possibly Ed

IDENTICAL twins Ed and Ted Miliband bring a fresh pair of faces to Gordon Brown's Cabinet. They are already known as the Ant and Dec of politics. But which one is which? One is brilliantly clever and so is the other one. One is to become Foreign Secretary. The other is to do some other job. One is married to a high-flying violinist. The other to a violin-playing trapeze artist *(Is this right? Ed.)*. Both have got 1000 legs *(You're fired, Ed.)*.

How will Gordon tell them apart when they say "That's a very good idea, Sir, much better than Tony ever had"?

Can you tell the difference between Ted and Ed? It's more fun than Sudoku!

Ed or possibly Ted

RISING STAR

ED BALLS, 17

Ed is the high-flying new education expert who is the first cabinet minister still to be at school. He is widely regarded as a "safer pair of balls" and is married to fellow cabinet minister and childhood sweetheart, Mini Cooper, 16¾.

THE BROON-ITES THE JOCKISH JUNTA THAT GENERATE GIGGLES!

GORDON BROON'S HIGHTAILED IT UP TAE BUCK HOUSE TAE HAVE A WEE GABBY WITH LIZ THA' SECOND...

SO MR BROON, HOW WOULD YOU LIKE TO FORM A GOVERNMENT FOR ONE?

WIST YER MOUTH, HEN...

AYE BEG YOUR PARDON?

HERE'S MA PROPOSITION. THE DEAL IS, YE STAY AS QUEEN FER A WEE WHILE, SMILE A WEE BIT, WEAR YER BAWBIES AND WAVE YER AULD HAND ABOUT...

THEN YE'LL STEP DOWN AN' BE AWA' AFTAE A FEW YEARS AND AH'LL TAKE OVER AS KING OF BRITAIN AN' BECOME THE HEID OF STATE!

UM... WHAT?

STRIDE!

PLEASURE DOIN' BUSINESS WITH YE, YER MAJ!

HENRY DAVIES

AH THINK THAT WENT VERY BRAW, DON'T YE?

JINGS!

GAWSH!

HOOTS!

PRIME MINISTERIAL DECREE NO. 1

From the Desk of the Supreme Leader

Comrades,

The Age of Change is upon us. We must all work together to achieve the changes that are required to build the new Britain of tomorrow.

That is why today I am announcing to you my first Five-Year Plan, which I have called 'A Five-Year Plan for the Age of Change in the New Britain'.

There are five key points in my Five-Year Plan, which are as follows:

1. An end to the highly dangerous personality cult which was allowed to grow up around the previous leader, Comrade Blair.

   No one had a greater respect for Comrade Blair than myself, and no one appreciates more warmly all that he did to advance the cause of the Party during his disastrous days in office.

   But we must acknowledge that mistakes were made. Many targets were not achieved. There was backsliding and a proliferation of capitalist deviationist errors involving the former leader and his entire household.

   I pledge that such lax standards will never be tolerated under the new regime of the Age of Change. Furthermore, those elements of the former regime known to have been involved in corrupt practices (such as Comrade Levy and Comrade Turner) will be arrested and made to stand public trial before being sentenced to the Gulag (ie Ford Open Prison).

   All images, statues and photographs of the former leader have been declared illegal as from midnight tonight, and will be forcibly removed.

   All elements who continue to express loyalty to the late leader will be incarcerated in prison, when we have built some more. (See Diktat No. 2 – 'British Prisons in an Age of Change'.)

2. Under the now universally discredited old regime, too much power was centralised into the hands of the former leader. Under the new regime in the Age of Change these powers will be returned where they belong – ie, to myself, representing the British people and the British Parliament.

   In honour of this historic return of power to the people, I hereby declare that a special day shall be designated, to be known as 'GB Day'.

   Flags will be issued to all British citizens, regardless of their gender, age, sexual orientation, ethnicity, creed, or willingness to wave them.

   The State declares that a condition of extreme gaiety and communal good humour shall prevail across the British nation for a period not exceeding 24 hours. (NB. There will be no smoking or drinking.)

3. The Party will mark the Age of Change by building 30 million new homes all over the British countryside to house the Polish workers who have had to be brought in to build the homes in the first place.

4. To encourage a healthy lifestyle in British womanhood, each pregnant female citizen will be issued with a one-off payment which must only be spent on the following traditional healthy items:
   British potatoes (not crisps)
   British cabbage
   British vodka (surely some mistake?)

5. I pledge that in the Britain of the Age of Change there will be an end to the outmoded principle of bourgeois sofa government. Hard chairs will be provided for all members of the Supreme Council of Ministers (formerly the Cabinet).

Agreed and ratified by myself (without any need for a referendum) as your Leader in the Age of Change.

Gordon Brown
Supreme Leader

That Very Important Newsnight Row In Full

(Serious music. Paxman turns to interview himself)

Paxman: So are you going to wear a tie?

Paxman: What I said was...

Paxman: Are you going to wear a tie?

Paxman: I think there are more important issues than...

Paxman: Are you going to wear a tie?

Paxman: The whole tie debate has moved on and...

Paxman: Just answer the question. Are you going to wear a tie?

Paxman: My record on ties is absolutely consistent...

Paxman: No, I'm sorry, I'm going to have to ask this one more time. Are you or are you not going to wear a tie?

Paxman: This is ridiculous. I'm not standing for this.

Paxman: Neither am I.

(Both rip off their ties and storm off in a huff)

"Look pal, that kind of ostentation was all very well in the Blair years, but this is the Brown era!"

MAN MIGHT BE GETTING BACK TOGETHER WITH GIRLFRIEND OR, THERE AGAIN, MIGHT NOT

STUNNING news emerged last night that a 25-year-old man and his ex-girlfriend are considering getting back together.

A source close to the ex-couple said, "Apparently he's, like, really up for seeing her again, but there again Portia, who's my best friend, reckons there's no way in a million years that they'll... *(cont. p. 94)*

WE WANT EVERYONE TO DO THEIR BIT!

LIVE EARTH

CLICK!

TELEVISION PRODUCERS IN MANIPULATION OF FOOTAGE TO MEET OWN TWISTED ENDS SHOCK

● Pope 'shits in woods'
● Bears 'Catholic'
● Er, wait a minute...

CONCERT FOR CAMILLA
'A Huge Success'

by Our Royal Staff **Lunchtime O'Bono**

A CONCERT to celebrate the birthday of Her Royal Highness Camilla The Not The Princess Of Wales attracted a huge crowd of five close friends in the front room at Highgrove. Among the stars performing for Camilla were the original Tetbury Foot Stompers (Bill Beard, trumpet; Wally Bovis, banjo; Ted Bingle, trombone and Miles Kington, double bass).

One guest, Lady Lobelia Lycett-Greenpeace, said that the concert had been "such fun" and "a really fitting tribute to a lovely lady"

WEMBLEY LATEST

THERE was shock today after a rock band took to the stage at Wembley not to remember Princess Diana, end global poverty or highlight the dangers posed by climate change.

Said the lead singer, "We just want to play our songs really loud, get drunk afterwards and sleep with *(cont. p. 94)*.

● Plans have been announced for a massive charity concert to remember Ricky Gervais's act dying tragically at the end of the Diana concert at Wembley. (Reuters)

BORIS PLAN FOR LONDON IN FULL

1. Blimey! Big place, London... Bit bigger than Henley-on-Thames but more or less the same sort of chap – river running through, shops, houses, lots of tourists...

2. One thing that is different is the underground railway thing! Haven't been on it yet because can't get my bike down the escalator. Sort that out pronto! In fact it'll be one of my big points – that'll knock Red Ken for six! "Bikes on the Tube." Yes, we could all cycle down the tunnels, damn sight safer than the roads, eh? You see, Ken hasn't thought of *that*, has he? Too busy sucking up to the commies and the gay chaps and so on...

3. One problem about London, though. Full of bloody Londoners! Self-pitying whingers, the lot of them. Even worse than Liverpool and Portsmouth. Always moaning about the tubes or the buses or the pigeons. Poor old Red Ken.

APOLOGY

Mr Boris Johnson would like to make it clear that he has the highest regard for the people of London and is second to none in his admiration for their dignity and courage (*as dictated by David Cameron*).

4. Now there was I? London, yes... The really good thing about London is all the top totty from all over the world! Cripes! Especially when the weather's a bit hot and they're not wearing much! Enough to make a chap fall off his bike if he's not careful!

Aaaarghhh!!

PRINCE HARRY

Your Royal Highness, we are extraordinarily grateful to you for giving up your valuable time to talk to us about spoons. And may I begin by asking you whether spoons have played an important part in your life?

Yeah, well, you know, speaking personally, I'd have to say, I mean, you know, whatever...

That's fascinating, Your Highness, and may I say again how thrilled we are to have you with us here on the Spoon column! Which brings me on to my second question: you are still a comparatively young man, but have you formed any attachment to a particular spoon that you would be willing to talk to us about?

Er, well, obviously, you know, these things are quite difficult to talk about. I mean, you've got to, really, you know, sort of...

That's wonderfully put, your Highness. And I can't help thinking at this point of your mother. Did she perhaps influence in any way your approach to spoons?

Well, yes, obviously, when you think about it, you know, I mean spoons, right, yeah... it's like how it is...

That's very moving, Your Highness, and I would like to thank you for sharing that very personal memory with us all. And may I end, as I always do, by asking you whether anything amusing has ever happened to you in connection with a spoon?

Yes, there was this night when we were all in Boujis, right, and Charlie Ricketson-Smythe drank, you know, three bottles of vodka and one of absinthe as a chaser, it was so funny, right, he got this spoon yeah and stuck it up Rupert's *(Sadly at this point a Royal Equerry intervened to explain that His Highness had been taken ill and would have to be returned to barracks immediately)*

NEXT WEEK: *Sir Alan Sugar – "Me and my sugar!"*

QUEEN OF PHOTOGRAPHERS FLIES INTO RAGE

by Our Royal Staff **Tina Brown**

HER Royal Highness Princess Anne of Leibowitz lost her temper yesterday when a silly old woman she was trying to photograph refused to do as she was asked.

A spokesman for the Princess said, "Annie is a very gracious lady, but she is not used to this lack of courtesy from one of her subjects.

"The protocol on these occasions is that the subject defers to the photographer. Men are expected to bow and women are expected to take off their crowns."

Queenie Fit

"On this occasion, the old woman stepped over the line of what is permissible and the Princess was perfectly entitled to explode with rage and put the silly old woman firmly in her place."

THE DAILY TELEGRAPH   Friday, July 20, 2007

Letters *to the Editor*

The Smoking Ban

SIR – Wherever I go in London these days, I find the streets packed with people engaged in the filthy habit of smoking.

Isn't it time there was a law to force these people only to smoke indoors, so that they do not inconvenience the rest of us with their disgusting, noxious, repulsive smoke?
Nick O'Tine
By email.

●Do you agree with Nick O'Tine? Or do you not smoke? Or perhaps you did once and now that you've given up you think smokers should be strung up because it's the only language they understand? We're not interested in your views but we've got a lot of space to fill up so please email us at once at readitontheblog@desperate.rubbish.telegraph.co.uk

POLICE PURSUE LIB DEM

We know it's you in there, Mr Kennedy

"Let's go inside – I can't stand the smoky atmosphere"

JUDGES NO LONGER TO WEAR TROUSERS

by Our Legal Correspondent **Harry Flashman**

IN THE biggest revolution in legal history, the Lord Chancellor has lifted the centuries-old requirement that judges must wear trousers when travelling on the train.

Justice Cockle-Out

In future, judges will be allowed to sit on the 8.13 to Waterloo wearing only their underpants so long as the said underpants conform to the Judicial Undergarment Propriety Code *(see Calvin v. Klein 1897)*.

Judges have generally welcomed the move. Said one, Justice Sir Ephraim Raincoat, "Seeing a judge all dressed up in trousers can sometimes be very intimidating for the public and they feel ill at ease. The new relaxed dress code should create a more informal atmosphere on the train where the judge is no longer a forbidding figure but is just like any other passenger, except not wearing any trousers."

● Pictures of the kind of trousers judges will no longer have to wear **94**

TORY REVEALED AS LABOUR SUPPORTER

by Our Political Staff **Simon Hogwarts**

THERE WAS huge embarrassment in the Conservative party last night when it was revealed that their candidate for Prime Minister was in fact a major supporter of Tony Blair.

Only two weeks ago, it was reported, David Cameron attended a function at the House of Commons where he went out of his way to encourage his supporters to give Mr Blair a standing ovation.

Tony Lite

Film showed a beaming Cameron clapping and cheering the Labour Prime Minister, and further research has shown that Mr Cameron once described himself to friends as "the heir to Blair."

Said a furious Tory backbencher Sir Simon Hefferlump, "Cameron is just an opportunist who has no real interest in politics and will say anything to get elected. And he's not even Asian."

A Doctor Writes

AS A doctor, I'm often asked, "Doctor, are you going to blow me up?"

The simple answer is "No, of course not." What happens is that the patient goes to see their doctor and notices that he has a foreign name and a beard.

At this point the patient experiences panic attacks, trembling, cold sweats and an urge to run away and return on Monday when old Dr Finlay is doing the surgery.

Normally, the patient has no cause for alarm, but in a very small number of cases the doctor, or *Terroristicus jihadicus normalis* to give it the full medical name, may indeed be a member of Al Qaeda. In these circumstances, the answer to the question may in fact be, "Yes, I'm afraid I am going to blow you up. Die, western infidel!"

If you are worried about your NHS doctor, go privately and you will be blown up much quicker. *(Is this right? Ed.)*

© A Doctor.

"It's not a secret terrorist message written in an Islamic script – it's my normal writing!"

TEENAGER ISN'T STABBED TO DEATH

SHOCKING news emerged last night when police announced that a teenager hadn't been stabbed to death in the UK within the last 24 hours.

A police spokesman said, "I must admit even the most hardened officers are today shocked by the fact that a youngster hasn't died in a horribly violent crime such as that which didn't occur."

Where are they now?

Tony Blair

FOR TEN years Tony Blair was the most powerful man in Britain. You could not open a newspaper or turn on the television without seeing his smiling face. But when he left office last week he quickly faded from memory and now few people can remember who he was or what he did. It is thought that he now spends his time doing good works in the Holy Land, although no one has seen him. *(Reuters)*

WANTED

Britain is on top-level 'critical' terrorist alert!

We are desperately searching for some policemen who might be able to save us from being blown up by lunatic Islamists.

The men we are looking for must fit the following profile:

1. When confronted with a bunch of convicted Somali murderers claiming to be visiting Pakistan for a 'backpacking holiday', they must not wave them goodbye with the words, "Have a nice day. Look forward to seeing you on your return when you come back with some harmless chemical souvenirs which you will carry with you on London Transport."

2. Er...

3. That's it.

DIARY

NANCY DELL'OLIO

I shall never forget the first time I met Sven. It was 1995. Barely out of my teenage years, my world was about to be changed forever.

It was at a very sophisticated party full of very, very important men, men of wisdom and experience, and their sadly resentful wives, who, behind their cold smiles, desperately yearned for the attention to fall upon them, not upon me.

Like a bolt from the sword of Thor, I felt those ice-blue Nordic eyes land on me from across the room. I was wearing a distinguished mini-skirt, with a tight open-top blouse overflowing with the grace and wisdom of my forebears.

I turned to see this brilliant, important man with the hard, thrusting spectacles of a Greek god.

I knew, as only a beautiful woman can, that in that split-second he was transfixed with a desire verging on obsession.

"How do you do" he said. "My name is Sven".

At this point, sex was out of the question. Was I not already happily married to someone else – a venerable old man with an extensive property portfolio?

But we must all follow our hearts, and where our heart leads us, sex will follow.

The man who called himself Sven put out his hand. Call it intuition, call it what you will, but I knew at that moment that what he desired most in the world was to shake it. And so I let him hold my hand and move it rhythmically up and down for seconds – seconds that to him must have seemed like hours.

I touched his hand. His hand touched mine. I was still in my teens.

Together we shook and shook and shook, until we could shake no more.

"May I be having the number of your telephone please for so as to contact you?" said Sven.

I could not hold back my tears!

This was madness!

But looking at Sven I could see that under that neat grey suit, a volcano was ready to erupt.

Without thinking, I wrote down my name on a piece of paper. As I did so, I noticed Sven's eyes following another woman – a woman dressed in a vulgar, attention-grabbing mini-skirt, anxious to sell her story for a vast amount of money – around the room. I had just finished writing my number when I heard Sven whisper to her:

"May I be having the number of your telephone please for so as to contact you?"

In that moment, my world was turned upside down. How could my Sven do this to me? My blood began to run hot and cold.

But my inner wisdom soon led me to the very heart of the matter, and within that wisdom I found much solace. You know what men are like! Yes! This was Sven's cry for attention: the more he chased after other women, the more desperate was his yearning for me! To me, Sven was a little boy who does something he knows will make his mother angry just to get her attention.

Without further ado, I held him by his ice-cold Nordic earlobe and led him kicking and screaming out of the room. As my venerable husband – or former husband, as he now was – watched us depart, he could not hold back the tears. Yes, I had once loved him – but as a Virgo my destiny lay elsewhere! I was eighteen years old, this was the end of the 1990s, and, with the World Cup beckoning, the world of international football was calling out for me.

When I heard the news of 9/11, shortly after my 21st birthday, I knew that these international terrorists would stop at nothing to get my attention.

I resolved then and there to bring about world peace. "With you by my side," I said to Sven in our luxury 5-star hotel suite, "I shall bring my never-ending quest for love and harmony to the world. Sven?...Sven?"

But Sven was nowhere to be seen. I eventually located him in the bathroom, where he was desperately trying to attract my attention by carrying on with the parlour-maid.

As a world, we are now also faced with the problem of climate change. The globe is growing hotter and hotter – and I blame myself. Are my dazzling designer outfits too sensual, too provocative? I must do whatever I can to calm it down, even if it involves the sacrifice of covering up my distinguished cleavage.

Yes, I have spent a lifetime searching for my personal meaning. My aim was to give to others, less fortunate than myself, a feeling of hope; and to bring about a global ceasefire.

I have achieved all these aims by agreeing to appear in full-colour photo-spreads in Hello! magazine on twelve separate occasions. Yes, it is hard work, but I am prepared to make these sacrifices for the rest of the human race. Sadly, I heard yesterday that the bitter fighting in Iraq has resumed. Once again, those insurgents are so upset that Sven has let me down. I do not hesitate. I telephone my good friend, the distinguished editor of OK!, and tell her that lives are at stake: there is nothing for it but an exclusive photoshoot in my skintight red silk dress with the plunging neckline. Ciao!

As told to CRAIG BROWN

OUT NOW!

The Latest Adventure Story From Hergé

HERGÉ

THE ADVENTURES OF TINTIN

TINTIN IN THE QUANGO

TINTIN, the boy reporter, embarks on his most comic caper yet when he is hauled up in front of the Commission for Racial Equality and is accused of being a racist. Will he escape? Will plain-clothes policemen Thomson and Thompson arrest everybody in Borders for selling material liable to incite the public to racial hatred? Why is Snowy white?

School news

St Cakes

St Coke's Day was held on July 11th. Mr P. Doherty was the guest speaker and gave out prizes in special silver foil. Parents were invited to look round Class 'A' Drug rooms and the Cannabis Garden, designed by Ms Rosie Boycott O.C. The traditional Drug of War contest between St Cokes and Harrow was cancelled after some contestants were caught trying to smoke the rope. There was a performance by the school orchestra of Elgar's Cocaine Overture in the Sir Keith Richard Memorial Hall. The Lower VIth put on a production of "An Inspector Knacker Calls" in the Daniella Westbrook Theatre. Spliffs were run over the Moss Meadow and several boys were arrested by the West Midlands police. The school song "Forty Grammes On" was sung in the chapel by the leavers under the Director of Music Sir Oswald "Ozzy" Osborne O.C. The school motto was then intoned by the new Head of Crack House, Rupert Street-Value (Needles), "Floreat Colombia". Passings out were on July 13th. Sentences were handed down on July 14th.

POETRY CORNER

Lines Written On The Retirement Of Mr Michael Aspel As Presenter Of The Antiques Roadshow

So. Farewell then
Michael Aspel.

You have been
Asked to leave
The Antiques Roadshow

Because you are now
So old that you
Have become
An antique yourself.

But you are not worth
Enough to be
On the
Show.

E.J. Thribb
(still 17½, so I can't be sacked!)

In Memoriam John Inman, Television Actor

So. Farewell
Then John
Inman.

Camp star of
Hit 1970s comedy
Are You Being Served?

"I'm free!"
That was your
Catchphrase.

And now
(In a very real sense)
You are.

E.J. Thribb (17½)

In Memoriam Eric Newby, Author

So. Farewell
Then Eric
Newby.

Celebrated travel
Writer.

Yes, you have
Chronicled many
Journeys to
Distant lands.

Now you
Are going
On the
Longest journey
Of all.

Eric Thribby (97¾)

POETRY CORNER

In Memoriam Lord Deedes, former Cabinet Minister and Editor of the Daily Telegraph

So. Farewell then
Bill Deedes,
Legendary journalist and
Tory politician.

"Shome mishtake shurely?"

That was your
Catchphrase.

But sadly there was
No mistake
About the news of your
Decease.

What will be your epitaph?

My suggestion is:
"Discontinued age 94."

E.J. Thribb (17½)

Lines on the Announcement of the Retirement of Tim Henman

So. Farewell
Then Tim
Henman,
Hero of
Wimbledon.

"Come on
Tim!"

That was
Our catchphrase.

But you
Never quite
Did.
E.J. Thribb (17½-15½)

In Memoriam Alan 'Fluff' Freeman, disc jockey

So. Farewell
Then pop
Pickers.

As you yourself
Might have
Said.

Sadly, your
Famous countdown
Has now
Reached
The end...

E.J. Thribb
(Number 17 and a "not 'arf")

W.F. Deedes
Notebook

WHEN I was a young man, the death of a mere journalist, however distinguished, would have attracted very little attention. In 1904, when I was a cub reporter on the Morning Post, I remember everyone on the paper was in a state of shock when our highly-respected editor Sir Ockinvole Crabtree-Blenkinsop dropped dead of a heart attack in the middle of our morning conference. No one batted an eyelid. His deputy, the very able P.R.J. Thistlethwaite immediately assumed the reins and instructed that this unfortunate event was not even to be reported in next day's edition. When I read the acres of newsprint which have been devoted in recent days to the demise of myself, it struck me how much things have changed in the course of the past hundred years.

Whether this is a change for the better or the worse, I will leave it to my readers to decide.

DUE to my new and unaccustomed status, I have lately acquired one of these new harps, which I am told in the right hands can make a very agreeable noise.

Alas, I have not yet mastered the instructions which, like so many things nowadays, come written in a great many different languages, few of which I have had the application to learn for myself over the years.

As a result, the sounds emanating from this particular cloud are not likely to find favour with the cognoscenti.

With a few million years of practise, however, the situation may well improve.

As to whether I am right, I leave that to my angelic audience to decide.

EXCLUSIVE TO ALL PAPERS

THE BILL DEEDES I KNEW

by EVERY HACK

I WILL never forget my one encounter with the legendary Bill Deedes.

We had both been sent to cover the 1987 Conservative Party conference in Blackpool.

When I arrived at the station, I saw the unmistakable figure of Bill Deedes, dressed in plus-fours and weighed down with a full set of golf clubs.

"I shay," he said in his inimitable drawl, "are you going to this conference affair?"

"Yes," I replied eagerly, looking forward to some sage insights into the inner machinations of the Tory hierarchy.

"Good," he responded. "Then you can help me with these clubs."

I think that said everything about the kind of man he was.

Now you can write your own Deedes tribute, even if you never met him! Just write the following sentences, in any order, and send to the *Daily Telegraph*, which will be delighted to print it.

● We shall never see his like again.

● He was the last of the gentleman journalists

● When they made Bill Deedes, they broke the mould.

● We shall never see his like again.

BLACKBERRYING 1957

BLACKBERRYING 2007

That Honorary Degree Citation In Full

SALUTAMUS SHILPAM SHETTIAM PULCHERRIMAM STELLAM INDIAM BOLLYWOODENSIS MULTITALENTA CANTANDO ET THESPIANO TERPSICHOROQUE SED FAMOSISSIMA IN "FRATRIS MAGNI" TELEVISIONIE REALITATE IN CANALE IV, VICTIMA GROTESQUE ABUSUS RACISTUS PER EXEMPLO 'POPPADUM' VOCATUM AUT 'PAKI' ETCETERA PER HIDEOSA ET GROSSA SLAGGA JADUM BONUM PROVOCAVIT IMMENSUM SCANDALUM GLOBALENSIS SED FELICITER FINALITER SHILPAM TRIUMPHAVIT IN DOMO "FRATIS MAGNI" GRATIA AD VOTO PUBLICO TELEPHONICO (RATUS PREMIUS AD XC DENARII PER MINUTEM) GAUDEAMUS IGITUR .

US GENERAL BLAMES BRITAIN FOR LOSING WAR

by Our US Military Correspondent **Buck Pass**

A TOP-RANKING US General last night pointed the finger of blame at the British Army for its failure to win the war in Vietnam.

"The limeys didn't do nearly enough in Vietnam. In fact, they weren't there at all."

He continued, "As a direct result of this feeble performance, we had no option but to evacuate Saigon and bomb Iran or was it Cambodia?"

MR GORDON BROWN
An Apology

IN RECENT months, in common with all other newspapers, we may have given our readers the idea that Mr Gordon Brown was totally unfitted to become the Prime Minister in succession to Mr Blair. Headlines such as "Dour Gordie is a Charisma-Free Zone", "Is Labour About To Make A Terrible Mistake?" and "With Boring Brown, Dave Will Walk The Next Election" may have conveyed the impression that we regarded Mr Brown as a grumpy, unimaginative Scottish loser whose premiership was doomed before it had even started.

We now recognise that there was not a jot or scintilla of truth in any of the above allegations, and would like to make it clear that Mr Brown's first weeks in office have been an unalloyed triumph, proving that he is a statesman of the first rank, whose honesty and sense of purpose shine out in dazzling contrast to the tawdry and meretricious duplicity of his predecessor. We have no hesitation in offering Mr Brown our sincere aplogies for any distress he may have been caused by our earlier reports.

© All newspapers.

HARRY POTTER
FACT FILE

Over 80 million copies of the latest Harry Potter book are being sold every second of the day.

The queue in Beijing for the new Harry Potter book was so long it could be seen from the moon.

Dumbledore is an anagram of Voldemort.

Daniel Radcliffe's glasses have been insured for $27 million.

If Hagrid were to wear Marks and Spencer chinos he would be an incredible size 94 (European 317).

The character of Professor Severus Snape is based on a real life academic – Professor David Starkey!

Harry Potter's favourite film is Lord of the Rings.

The word "Muggle' comes from the Anglo-Saxon word "Muglõr" meaning "Trouserpress".

Alastair Campell records in his diary seeing Prime Minister Tony Blair reading Harry Potter out loud to President George Bush – wearing only yellow and green underpants.

In the final book Hermione is revealed as a direct descendant of Mary Magdalen with a divine bloodline preserved by the Order of the Merovingian Pheonix and the Brotherhood of the Priory of Opus Sesame.

More than 11,000 Harry Potter Fact Files are published in newspapers every day in a desperate attempt to fill up space and cash in on *(That's enough Potter facts, Ed.)*

"180 quid that Nintendo wii cost me! And you're reading a bloody book!"

'WHY WON'T THESE JOURNALISTS LEAVE MADDY'S PARENTS ALONE?'

by Our Man Keeping The Story Going **Al Garve**

THE tearful, lined faces tell their own story. The agony is etched in every feature. And the final twist of the knife for the tortured parents of little Maddy has been the outrageous behaviour of the Portuguese press.

For weeks, these irresponsible and callous so-called journalists have been indulging in a daily orgy of speculation without a shred of evidence to support their poisonous guesswork.

No story is too wild for these heartless hacks to repeat ad nauseam, no theory too ridiculous for them to splash over their front pages.

They have even now pointed their malodorous fingers at the McCann parents themselves, incredibly suggesting that they themselves might have been involved in the little girl's disappeareance or, heaven forbid, her death.

How dare these vile foreign muck-rakers continue to peddle their endless obsessive stream of innuendoes and filth in a desperate bid to promote the circulation of their revolting apologies for newspapers.

Don't they realise that that is our job?

On Other Pages

● Is Maddie story still alive? Fears grow **2-94**

PLUS Free poster featuring a picture of Maddy, carrying the urgent message 'Read the Sun/Express/Mail/Independent' (or any other paper of your choice).

"Mr Morrison, I'm not going to take any chances. Your test appears to show you to be one of the undead"

Record Poppy Crop In Afghanistan*

*and Iraq

ENEMIES OF REASON
Part 94

(Silly music. Elderly donnish figure wearing casual clothes and expression of deep concern gazes earnestly into camera)

Professor Richard Dawkins *(for it is he)*: It is frightening to think that in the 21st century there are millions of people all over the world who believe that they can change the future by a simple act involving a birthday cake.

(Cut to shot of family group clustered around Marks & Spencer chocolate cake covered in lit candles. Woman blows out candles while the rest of her family shout 'Go on, Mum – make a wish!" Close-up of woman with eyes closed, accomanied by sinister music. Cut to Dawkins, looking shocked and incredulous)

Dawkins *(interviewing woman)*: Mrs Simpkins, can I ask you what you think you were doing just now?

Mrs Simpkins: Well, I just made a wish while I was blowing out the candles, like I always do.

Dawkins: And you really thought that what you were wishing for would in some mysterious way come true?

Mrs Simpkins: Well, you never know, do you?

Dawkins: But how could blowing out candles on a cake have any influence over a future event? Isn't that just the most crude, primitive, infantile, unscientific superstition?

Mrs Simpkins: Well, if you're going to be like that, you're not going to have any of my cake.

Dawkins: As a control test, tell me what it is you wished for?

Family: Don't tell him, Mum, or it won't come true.

Dawkins *(to camera)*: So obviously the followers of this cult are under a vow of silence not to divulge the object of the "wish", to prevent any analysis of the outcome of their pathetic ritual, thus exposing it as an empty and futile act of self-deception for insecure neurotics.

(Cut to men in white coats looking through microscopes at pieces of birthday cake)

Dawkins: For the last five years, a team of researchers from the University of New Dworkins has been analysing over 2,000 case histories of the Birthday Wish cult. The leader of the team, Professor Hiram Moonbat, gave me his findings.

Bearded Scientist: In examining 2,522 samples, we could find little or no correlation between the expression of the "wish" by the anniversarial celebrant and any ultimate wished-for event.

Dawkins: Well, that proves it, doesn't it? The whole thing is rubbish, isn't it? And it is deeply alarming that, in the 21st century, the dark forces of unreason should still have so many millions of people in their grip, still indulging in...

Professor Moonbat *(in background)*: ... however, our researchers were somewhat hampered by the fact that no one would tell us what they had wished for, which rather invalidated...

Dawkins *(intervening)*: So there we have it, Everyone in the world is mad except me, and very, very dangerous.

(Cut to shot of birthday cake exploding, destroying family home. Caption reads "Reconstruction")

NEXT WEEK: Professor Dawkins looks at the bizarre practice of shooting fish in a barrel, concluding that it is deeply unscientific and boring to watch.

The Nation's Favourite View

Sir Trevor McDonald goes in search of Gryf Rhys-Jones up a mountain driven in a vintage car by Robbie Coltrane. Will he find Sir David Dimbleby looking for Neil Oliver on the coast? Or will he fly off to India instead to meet Sanjiv Bhaskar looking for Victoria Wood in the footsteps of Michael Palin?

Eye rating: Z-z-z-z-z

IT'S THE COLD PHWOARR!

I'm flexing my missiles

GLENDA SLAGG

FLEET STREET'S FISH WIFE!!!

■ **CHRIS TARRANT??!?** Who Wants To Bed A Millionaire??!?? (Geddit?!!?) Not me, mister, when he comes home stinking of fish and needs a bucket of Viagra to get started!!??!! Poor old Ingrid – that's Mrs Tarrant that was, stoopid – no wonder she decided to phone a lawyer and take the money!!??? Geddit??!?? She *didn't* geddit very often 'cos her two-timing' hubby was too busy a-jumpin' and a-humpin' anything in a skirt!!????

■ **INGRID TARRANT** – arent-chasickofher!?!? OK, so your hubby comes home stinking of fish and needs a bucket of Viagra to get started!???! Who wouldn't if they were married to an old ratbag like you???!? Let's face it, darling, you wanted to be a millionaire, but you couldn't answer the simplest question, ie where was your hubby last night??? Phone a friend??!? You haven't got any, love, that's why you phoned up the Daily Mail instead!!!?!

■ **AMY WINEHOUSE??!?** Dontchaluvher???!? She's the female Pete Doherty who has cheered us through the dark days of summer by getting stoned and legless and not turning up for her own concerts!!?! Good on yer, Amy – don't let them spoil the fun by sending you to Rehab!!?! Geddit???!? You just go down the Wine House and get good and pissed!!??!

■ AMY WINEHOUSE!!?! What a disgrace!!! What kind of role model does she make for Britain's kids, a-boozin' and a-floozin' all over the papers as if she was Pete Doherty in a dress??!? Take a tip from Auntie Glenda – get yourself down to Rehab (Geddit??!) before you end up in the Mad House!??! Geddit???!??

Byeeee!!!

LATEST EMBARRASSING TARRANT REVELATIONS

I wasn't impressed by his tackle

POLICE LOG

Neasden Central Police Station

0815 hrs All officers assembled in canteen for working breakfast to assess the assignment of the entire Neasden force to the Climate Change Protest Camp at Heathrow. Officers equipped with calculators reported that this would result in a total of 4,812 hours overtime for the Neasden force. This would represent a welcome £1.2 million uplift in officers' income, but would sadly necessitate a reallocation of budgetary resources, resulting in the closure of the station on alternate Mondays, Wednesdays and Thursdays.

1015 hrs An armed response unit was deployed to the head office of Channel Four Television, following the broadcasting of a documentary film entitled "Lunatic Islamo-Fascists At Large". The film had shown footage of clerics exhorting their followers to "Kill the Jews", "String Up the Poofs", "Stone the Shameless Women who Expose Their Faces in Public" and "Behead All Infidels Now".

The officers arrested the makers of the film under the Anti-Muslim Discrimination Acts 2001, 2004, 2005 and 2007, for wilfully attempting to incite racial hatred by showing footage of people inciting racial hatred. Employees of the television station unfortunately were caught in the crossfire, resulting in a number of fatalities.

1500 hrs CCTV operator demands assistance as two female suspects in the Nkomo Lido remove their upper garments to reveal their bare chests. A call for volunteers was answered by all male officers and some female ones.

2325 hrs Calls received from various members of the public alleging that a major battle had broken out on the Tabo Mbeki Estate between rival gangs of 11-year-olds fighting a "turf war" related to crack cocaine dealing, involving knives, handguns and AK47s. The callers were played a recording of the recent press conference by Chief Constable Sir Ian Knacker, calling for communities to take responsibility for the activities of their children and not to expect his officers to waste valuable police time dealing with crime.

"You've over-charged your taser again, Rawlings"

Duchess of Tears

by DAME SYLVIE KRIN, author of *Love In The Saddle, Born To Be Queen, Heir of Sorrows,* etc etc.

THE STORY SO FAR: Charles and Camilla are visiting the Gloucestershire village of Trelford-under-Water to see for themselves the extent of recent flood damage.

Now read on...

IT REALLY is appalling!" Charles peered from the bow of the Royal Dinghy *Britannia* and pointed to the spire of St Levy's church, just visible above the swirling flood. Overhead a helicopter hovered, lifting two stranded pensioners and a sheep to safety

"And look, Camilla! Over there! Look at those people sitting on that rooftop. Wave to them, darling! It'll mean a lot to them."

Struggling unsuccessfully to open her multi-coloured golfing umbrella (a present from Mr Abdul Hatterji, proprietor of the Jet Service Station and 24-Hour Mini-Mart at Stroud), Camilla obligingly waved a gloved hand towards the unfortunate looters.

"There, you see!" beamed Charles triumphantly. "They're giving you the V-sign. It's just like the war when Grandfather visited the East End after the bombing."

"This umbrella's useless," Camilla moaned, hurling the brolly in a fit of frustration into the rising tide and watching it as it was swept away. "No wonder they're giving them away free."

But Charles seemed oblivious to her discomfort. "I know it's really ghastly for everyone to be flooded and see all their furniture swept away. But, on the other hand, this sort of thing really brings out the best in the British nation."

WITHIN minutes Charles and Camilla reached their destination – an improvised pontoon tethered to the forecourt of the local Tesco where a vast group of newsmen and photographers were waiting. Film crews clung to treetops, their cameras precariously balanced on the broken branches.

"Leave this to me, old thing," Charles whispered to Camilla as they waded towards the waiting microphones. "You see, they'll want me to say something to boost morale. It's expected of one."

"Gentlemen," he began. "This flood thingy. It really is appalling..." But he could get no further as the throng of newsmen pressed towards Camilla, thrusting their microphones towards her perfectly formed lips.

"Over here, Cammy!" shouted the rubicund-featured Bill Grozzer, the *Daily Telegraph*'s highly respected Court Correspondent. "This big 10th anniversary service for the People's Princess – are you going to go, love? Or are you afraid of being booed off the stage?"

Charles watched in horror as question followed question like shafts of poisoned darts and Camilla struggled like a wounded deer to defend herself.

"I... er..." she stuttered in vain. But her faltering response was lost in a tumultuous clap of thunder and the heavens opened yet again.

● Download the GnomeAudio version of this Sylvie Krin story read by Dame Judi Dench from our website – www.gnometrash.co.uk.

---

10 BEST BUYS
SANDBAGS

1. 'Homedry'

This basic, easy-to-handle bag, weighing 24.32 kilograms, won the Environment Agency's 2006 'Sandbag of the Year' award.
Price: £10.99

2. 'Blitz Spirit'

This World War Two model is an exact reproduction of the sandbags used by Dad's Army to hold back Hitler's hordes. **Price: Half-a-Crown (2/6)**

3. 'Greensand'

This eco-friendly sandbag, woven from sustainable palm  fronds, is filled with Fairtrade sand from the Sahara Desert. Recommended by Greenpeace and Friends of Sand.
Price: £25.99

4. 'The Royal Sandringham'

This luxurious sandholder comes with a five-year guarantee from the Duchy of Cornwall. Will withstand tsunami-style floods for up to 15 years. **Price: £250**

5. 'Just-A-Bag'

Best of the economy range, this fill-your-own bag is made from recycled copies of the *Daily Telegraph*. The makers say, "What you see is what you get. This is a no-frills bag. All you have to do is fill it with sand."

★ **Eye Best Buy** ★
Price: 3p for 1000

6. 'La Serenissima'

As used for centuries by rich Venetians to protect their palazzos, this classic Renaissance design has been given a modern twist by top Italian designer Sandi Bagatti. Made from porous ground coral, the bag absorbs water for up to 20 minutes before dissolving in a sustainable manner and floating away. **Price £1,250**

(That's enough sandbags. Ed.)

Full list of stockists p. 94

WETTEST SINCE RECORDS BEGAN

by Our Westminster Correspondent
Michael Trenchfoot

SENIOR Tories have announced that a disaster-prone June and July has confirmed that David Cameron is officially the wettest leader of the party since records began in 1752.

"Will that be all, Sir?"

FLOODS – 'ALL GOD'S FAULT' SAY CHILDREN OF ISRAEL

from Our Man On The Ark **G. RAAF**

AS rain beat down for the 40th day running, millions of homeowners saw their properties finally vanishing below what they were calling "the worst floods since the world began".

One question was going up on every side as angry drownees were engulfed by the fast-rising waters – "Why, oh why were we not given proper warning of this disaster so that we could have taken proper life-saving precautions?

"We blame God for failing to alert us to this deluge, which is now covering the earth to a depth of 36 cubits."

However, a spokesman for the Almighty was quick to point out that He had given plenty of warnings, and that the only person who had heeded them was the world-famous ecologist Mr Noah.

Ham & High Ground

Mr Noah, 912, told drowning newsmen last night that he had been predicting the rising water level for over one hundred years.

"Anyone," he said, "could have done what I did – namely build an Ark and fill it with two members of every species of creature, so that biodiversity can be preserved in a post-flood situation."

● Why, oh why do you think the entire human race seems to have built its homes on a flood plain, except Noah? We'd like to hear from you, via raven or dove.

HALF THE CABINET ADMITS 'YES, WE DID TRY SOCIALISM'

by Our Political Staff **Mary Juana and Harry Pot**

FOLLOWING the admission of Home Secretary Jacqui Smith that she had "experimented with left-wing politics" while at university, seven of her fellow Cabinet ministers rushed to confess that they had done the same.

Said one minister, Ruth Kelly, "It was just something everyone did in the '70s. I can remember going to these parties where everyone was wearing CND badges and quoting from Paul Foot's latest column in the *Socialist Worker*.

"I don't mind admitting that I did it quite a few times," she went on, "and it did give me a bit of a buzz. But I wasn't an addict – no way."

Keep Off The Grass

Said another senior Cabinet minister, Alistair Darling, "Socialism was quite harmless, in my view. A lot of us were into it in those days. But when we all came down from University and met Tony Blair, we realised that we didn't need it any more."

● Did you smoke socialism at university? If so, we'd like to hear from you. And so would PC Yates, now that he's got nothing better to do with his time. Text or email us at www.dailytelegrass.co.uk

"I think you've taken Chiaroscuro to its limits, Caravaggio!"

The Alternative Rocky Horror Service Book

No. 94 A memorial service to celebrate the 10th Anniversary of the death of a much-loved Princess

The Archbishop of Canterbury *(for it is he)***:** Your Majesty, Lord Spencer, Mr Fayed, ladies and gentlemen. We are gathered together, at least those of us who have been invited, to commemorate the life of the late Princess of Wales.

Congregation: She was the People's Princess.

Mr Fugger *(from the pews)***:** What about my fuggin' son?

The President: I was just coming to that bit. We also remember at this time all the other ones who weren't so famous but whose lives were so tragically cut short by this terrible accident.

Mr Fugger: It was fuggin' murder! The Duke of Edinburgh did it!

(The Duke of Edinburgh will remain seated or he may kneel)

Congregation: Shadd-up-your-face, Fugger, and siddown!!

(There will then follow an address by Earl Spencer)

Spencer: Whilst it has never been proved that the Duke of Edinburgh murdered my sister, it is the sort of thing he would have done, given half a chance. Bloody Windsors! In the meantime, I would like to remind you that the Althorp Diana experience is open throughout the summer at the very modest price of £50 per head – regrettably, there are no concessions, but visitors will be given a personal tour by myself and my delightful new partner. Amen.

Prince Harry: Where do you get a drink round here?

Prince William: Yah.

(There shall then follow a piece of popular music rendered by Sir Elton of John or it may be Sir George Michael of Wham)

Prayers

(Prayers will then be led by the Prince of Wales. The congregation will make the response "It really is appalling" at the appropriate juncture)

Charles: Dear God, you know, this whole death thingie is just, you know, so upsetting for all of us and ten years is a jolly long time and the press go on and on about it as though it was yesterday, it's pretty hard on Camilla who's made a good fist of it really. I mean, when you think about it...

All: It really is appalling.

Charles: So I think the best thing for everyone really is to put the whole thingie behind us and move on. Amen.

(The congregation will then sing the traditional hymn composed by St Gerald and the Pacemakers)

Move on! Move on!
With hope in your hearts
And you'll never think about Di again!
You'll never think about her again.

(Flowers wrapped in cellophane will then be placed on the altar by representatives of all faiths as the congregation leaves to be photographed by waiting paparazzi.

The organ will play Bach's Toccata and Fugoff)

© The Church of England 2007.

GREAT WHITE SPACE SPOTTED

by Our August Staff Phil Space

A HUGE white space was seen last night in the middle of our newspaper to the horror of the editor and the shocked staff.

The space, which was at least 9 inches long and over 6 inches wide was believed to be floating about where sensible news items are normally put.

Luckily at the last minute emergency journalists filled the space with ridiculous items about non-existent sharks and the discovery of Lord Lucan for the 100th time.

A relieved editor told readers, "Thank goodness for complete rubbish. Without it that great white space could have been very dangerous – if not lethal."

"*I'm sorry, sir... I can't discuss individual cases*"

POLLY FILLER'S

HOLIDAY COLUMN

HELLO. My name Serfina from Grotsk. Mrs Polly and useless Simon go holiday in Dubai or "You Buy" as Mrs Polly say but I no understand joke?

So Mrs Polly leave me big list things to do.

1. Wash useless Simon underpants – remember not in microwave, stupid girl.

2. Don't eat everything in fridge or cupboard or you go back to Grotsk eat potato see how you like that.

3. Write column for newspaper. Easy peasy. No take long.

4. Sit in room feel homesick and cry. No, just joke says Mrs Polly!

5. Look after toddler Charlie. he too young go Dubai. Much better he stay here and annoy you. Take him Harry Potter film – which Serfina do every day!!

6. Pack bags and clean out room ready to be sacked when Mrs Polly return in bad mood because useless Simon spend whole holiday watching Pro-Celebrity Dwarf Camel Racing from Abu Dhabi with James May on Al Jazeera Extreme Sport 3.

So I must go now, Charlie pretend be wizard and set fire to hamster!?!

Gudbye!

© Serfina Svetshopski
pp Polly Filler 2007.

What's So Wrong With Slugs?

Asks Max Hastings

THIS year's wet summer has had one very obvious consequence – a huge increase in the number of slugs in our gardens.

And to hear some people go on, you'd think that this was some kind of a disaster.

We're told that the slugs are eating all our precious flowers and vegetables and leaving our gardens looking like some sort of wasteland.

Keep Going

What nonsense! Agreed, the slug may not be one of the most handsome of our God's creatures – black and slippery, leaving a trail of slime wherever he goes.

He cannot be compared, I grant it, to a gorgeous, multi-coloured butterfly or a grouse.

And, of course, grouse have the great advantage that they can be shot and eaten – whereas few of us in our right mind would look forward to tucking into a plate of roast slug and chips!

Is This Right?

And no one, I admit, is going to be too happy to find all their prized nasturtiums eaten to the bone by these marauding pests.

But to my mind there is one good reason above all others for singing the praises of Johnny Slug...

And that is because you're being paid a couple of grand by my old friend Paul Dacre to dash off something that will get Middle England talking!

© *Dacretrash Productions.*

THAT ALL PURPOSE CELEBRITY DRUGGIE PIECE IN FULL

by Our Showbiz Staff **Phil Nostrils**

LAST NIGHT friends of Amy/Pete/Kate/Lindsay were concerned as the troubled singer/model/actress dramatically booked themselves back/took themselves out of rehab.

Looking pasty, thin and tired, Amy/Pete/Kate/Lindsay flicked a V sign at reporters before going in/coming out of a nightclub at three o'clock in the morning.

Said friends of Amy/Pete/Kate/Lindsay, "she/he is trying hard to get their life back together but the pressures of the business have taken their toll."

Other friends fear that Amy/Pete/Kate/Lindsay are struggling to avoid the bad influence of their husband/girlfriend/boyfriend/bloke she just met in the club.

"It's a tragedy waiting to happen," said yet another friend, "and we just pray that Amy/Pete/Kate/Lindsay doesn't go the way of Janis/Kurt/Sid/Judy/Marilyn/whoever/although it doesn't matter since no-one is going to get to the end of this piece anyway."

To The Editor of Ants and Antmen

Dear Sir,

In answer to all those readers who have been troubled by a plague of unwanted Daily Telegraphs, may I recommend the solution urged by my late grandfather.

Whenever he came across an unwanted copy of the newspaper in question, he poured boiling water all over it. That soon solved the problem!

Minnie Arkwright
Heckmondwyke

Dear Sir,

In our family we stopped the Daily Telegraph getting into our house by putting Sellotape over the letterbox. A cheap and highly effective answer to the problem!

The Duke of Westminster
Cheshire

Dear Sir,

I am sorry to confess after 60 years that when at my prep school we were confronted with an infestation of Daily Telegraphs, we used a magnifying glass to concentrate the rays of the sun on the unfortunate newspaper until it burst into flames. It may sound cruel but it certainly sorted out the problem!

Peregrine Worsthorne
Basildon

GCSE TABLES
How Your Newspaper Fared

	A	B	M	F	U
Telegraph	37	98%	32%	94in	1,732,000
Times	42	84%	24%	38cm	874,000
Mail	94	72%	17%	36m	532,000
Guardian	17	1%	342%	42cc^2	2
Independent	58	3%	N/A	37 hectares (Kent only)	None
Sun	7	-5%	43° F	1 yard	Page 3
Mirror	3	-3%	-15° C	Grapefruit Segments	Don't Know

Explanation of Table

A = Number of pictures of fruity girls leaping in air.
B = Percentage of pieces saying GCSEs have been dumbed down.
M = Percentage of editorials saying "Leave our kids alone".
F = Column inches devoted to Asian four-year-old who has got 27 A*s.
U = Number of readers who have deserted in desperation at number of incomprehensible space-filling GCSE tables.

UCAS Clearing
An Eye Service To Readers

Places Still Available

University of Lunn

(formerly Lunn Poly)

Facebook Studies, 4-year course including practical communication modules: talking to friends, posting pictures of self at Reading Festival, and compiling lists of Most Shaggable Members On Course.

(formerly Pretty Polly)

Advanced Domestic Science, 33-year course: How to live with your parents for the rest of your life and stop them renting your room out

The Metropolitan University of Toynbee

(formerly Toynbee Polly)

Football Management, 1-year course – may be curtailed to 2 matches depending on week-by-week results

(That's enough courses. Ed.)

⚠️

HOUSE OF LORDS COMMITTEE INTERNET WARNING

1. Repeatedly typing in 'goople' is a complete waste of time.

2. The man on the other end of the help-line in India gets very stroppy after the eighth time that you've failed to find the on button on the front of the computer.

3. You do not win a million dollars if you click those pictures that pop up from nowhere. You just get more pop-up pictures.

4. If you repeatedly type 'hot-males' into your search engine you do not see that email from your children on holiday in Australia, but you do get very funny looks from your wife when she next uses the bloody thing.

"Have you tried this? It used to be all the rage"

Hitler's Desert Island Discs Found

by Our Classical Music Staff
Hugh Trevor-Ropey (formerley Lord Paul Dacre)

MORE THAN 60 years after Hitler's death, a Soviet archivist has revealed a cardboard box, looted by a Soviet soldier from the Fuehrer's bunker, containing eight 78rpm records in perfect condition.

Incredibly, it seemed, the Fuehrer had spent the war years planning which records he would select when, after conquering Britain, he would order Mr Roy Plumley to invite him to appear on his celebrated Desert Island Discs programme.

Deutsche Gramophon Uber Alles

Surprisingly, Hitler included only one record by his beloved Wagner among the eight he would take to the imaginary island.

And even more astonishing was his inclusion on his list of a number of Jewish composers and performers.

That list in full:
1. *The Meister-race Singers* (Wagner)
2. *Fiddler On The Roof* (Yehudi Menuhin's greatest Hits)
3. *Theme tune from Genevieve* (played by Larry Adler on the harmonica)
4. *Main title from The Benny Goodman Story* (featuring Benny Goodman)
5. *The George Gershwin Songbook* (Sammy Davis Jnr.)
6. *Barbra Streisand Live At Carnegie Hall*
7. *Elgar's Pomp and Circumcised No. 4* from The Last Night of the Pogroms
8. *Hitler On The Roof Medley* including *"If I Were a Reich Man"* by Topol

Also in the cardboard box was Hitler's luxury, a lox bagel with cream cheese (but not too much gherkin) and his favourite book The Autobiography of Groucho Marx.

You can now hear Hitler's Hits by downloading the podcast from www.DerTelegraphFuehrer Favourites.co.uk

---

PRODUCT RECALL

WE regret that serious faults have been detected in our popular Chinese figurine 'Ming', which has necessitated its urgent withdrawal from the market. We have received a number of complaints about this model, in particular its high leaden content, which has rendered it unfit for purpose. Following tests suggesting that 'Ming' could cause the death of the Lib Dem party, we are planning to replace this obsolete product with a new and entirely safe version. Details to be announced shortly.

THE McCANNS
An Apology

IN COMMON with all other newspapers we may have given the impression that we considered Kate and Gerry McCann to be model parents distraught with grief caught up in a nightmare beyond imagination. Headlines such as 'The Grief Of The McCanns', 'The Saddest Sorrow' and 'Prayers For The Suffering Couple' may have led readers to believe that our sympathy lay with the desperate and despairing parents of the missing toddler.

We now realise that these comments may well have been premature and that actually we had a niggling feeling all along that there was something a bit funny about them... just a bit too calm really... and all that going to see the Pope... could have been a smokescreen... I mean we're not saying she did it but who else could it have been and as for the DNA you can't fake that can you and what about the sniffer dogs, they're not going to be wrong are they?

In the light of the above considerations we would like to apologise to Mr and Mrs McCann for our earlier insinuations of their innocence.

TOMORROW: An Apology for the above Apology.

MADDIE: The Unanswered Questions

1. Why don't we know anything?
2. Why do we give so much space to something we know nothing about?
3. Isn't there anyone who has a clue what's going on?
4. Will we ever know anything?
5. When are we going to stop asking the unanswered questions?

MADDIE: The Timetable in Full

8.57 Editor asks hacks "What have we got on Maddie?"
9.00 Hacks turn on Sky TV for latest broadcast from Portugal.
9.04 Hacks desperately do Google search on "Maddie".
9.08 Editor throws tantrum.
9.12 Chief sub comes up with headline "MADDIE – THE UNANSWERED QUESTIONS".
9.15 Paper goes to bed.
9.16 Hacks go to the pub.

Radio 4
What You Missed

Jim Naughtie: The sleepy little Leicestershire village of Rothley has never seen anything like it. An appalling media circus has descended like a plague of locusts on this sleepy little village in Leicestershire. Our reporter Phil Airtime is there now. Phil, what can you tell us?

Phil: Well, Jim, the people of the sleepy Leicestershire village of Rothley have been woken up by an appalling media circus that has descended like a plague of locusts on this sleepy Leicestershire village.

Naughtie: So, what's the scene there, Phil?

Phil: Well, I can see literally hundreds of reporters from all over the world reporting on how the appalling media circus has descended like a plague of locusts on this sleepy Leicestershire village.

Naughtie: And what's the feeling there amongst the local people, Phil?

Phil: Well I'm just ringing the doorbell of one of the sleepy villagers now.

(Sound of doorbell ringing)

Good morning, sir, how do you feel about the invasion of your sleepy little village by an appalling media circus? Do you think that they are like a plague of locusts?

(Sound of violent scuffle)

Naughtie: Oh dear, we seem to have lost Phil there. So now it's time for Thought for the Day and our speaker today is the Chief Imam of the Bluewater Mosque, Jihad Al Q'aeda-Smith.

Imam: Good morning Jim. Well, I was coming here this morning on the bus and I thought to myself, "Wouldn't it be a good idea to blow it up?" And, you know, in a real sense, perhaps we all of us have a duty to
(cont. 94 kHz)

FRIDAY, AUGUST 31, 2007

WILL FALL IN HOUSE PRICES CAUSE FALL IN HOUSE PRICES?

By Our Property Staff
Clare Munger

THERE were fresh fears of a total collapse in the housing market after it was revealed that dangerously high levels of Chinese lead had been discovered unlabelled on Home Information Packs which are thought to be responsible for the outbreak of saucy BBC newsreaders flashing their thighs on the nightly news, which experts warn will almost certainly lead to the end of civilisation as we know it, as the nation descends into anarchy and *(cont. p. 94)*

Why the markets are in turmoil

Our Economics Editor explains

By D.O.W Jones

The recent fall in the equity markets was sparked by a crisis of confidence in the American sub-prime mortgage sector which exposed a number of hedge fund and private equity leveraged consolidated debt deals to pressure from er...er...er. **Full story page 94**

Your questions answered

Q Will house prices go up?

A In the short term, it looks unlikely with a correction to the property market caused by interest rate level fluctuations, but in the long term this may herald a flight from equities back into property which would er...er...certainly do something or other...

Q Will my pension be affected?

A Yes and no. Dealers are now looking to Japan where any movement in government bonds geared to mortgage debt reassessment could well trigger a run on grapefruit segments *(is this right, Ed?)*

Q Do you *really* understand this?

A No. No-one does.

VICTORIOUS TROOPS RETREAT FROM BASRA

by Our Man On A Flight Home To London **Dan Kirk**

TONIGHT I saw with my own eyes one of the most glorious moments in the history of the British Army, as it retreated in triumph in the middle of the night from Basra.

Blenheim, Waterloo, St Pancras and now... Basra. This is the roll-call of honour that will live for ever in the minds of generations of schoolchildren.

A lone bugle sounded the advance, which marked the end of one of the most heroic and successful campaigns in the history of the British Army. *(You've done this bit. Ed.)*

In 2003, the British marched into Basra with bands playing and heads held high, bent on bringing democracy, law and order to a war-torn land.

Four years later, their task was completed. As the Commanding Officer, General

Withdrawal, told me yesterday, "We've now got to the point where we can hand over the city quite safely to the Shi-ite militias. They are very well trained by the Iranians and have done a splendid job in killing our chaps *(Don't put that in, old boy... bad for morale!)*".

Within an hour of leaving Basra, our victorious troops were rapidly advancing to the airport ready for the final surge back to Heathrow.

For free Gnome 'Victory In Basra' plate offer, see p. 94

Advertisement

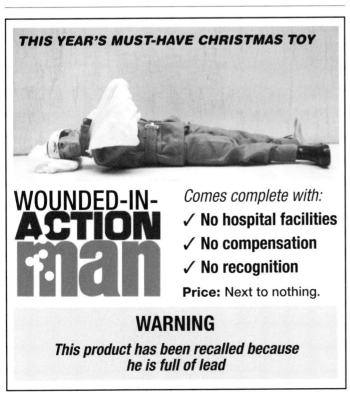

"Martin, come in. Listen, I'm looking for someone to take over Robert's department"

Mrs Shakespeare
by Germaine Greer

MALE scholars have always assumed wrongly that Shakespeare was a man. All the evidence suggests that the plays were in fact written by a strong, independent, possibly Australian woman living with a lot of ducks near the M11.

Consider the play "Ozello", the tragic story of a brilliant feminist author who comes to England and is murdered by jealous male critics who *(cont'd p94)*

The New Modern Bestseller

Over 1 million copies stolen

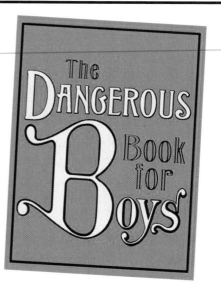

Contents

Chapter One: Turning your tree house into a crack den

Chapter Two: Hot wiring a Porsche, BMW or Mercedes

Chapter Three: The AK47. Its history and modification

Chapter Four: Great gangs of England

Chapter Five: Breeding pit bulls for fun and profit

Chapter Six: Songs for singing round the fire (car, house, school, etc). A selection of stirring rap anthems including "Fuk Tha Fukkin Fukka"

Chapter Seven: A guide to stolen Rolexes – all the whys and wherefores

Chapter Eight: Heroic Lives – Alfonso Stiletto, inventor of the Flick Knife

Chapter Nine: How to cook for yourself with only a Pot Noodle and a microwave

Chapter Ten: Posting threatening videos on YouTube *(That's enough. Ed.)*